A Critique of Provisionism

A Critique of Provisionism

A Response to Leighton Flowers's "The Potter's Promise"

Matthew Cserhati

WIPF & STOCK · Eugene, Oregon

A CRITIQUE OF PROVISIONISM
A Response to Leighton Flowers's "The Potter's Promise"

Copyright © 2024 Matthew Cserhati. All rights reserved. Except for brief quotations in critical publications or reviews, no part of this book may be reproduced in any manner without prior written permission from the publisher. Write: Permissions, Wipf and Stock Publishers, 199 W. 8th Ave., Suite 3, Eugene, OR 97401.

Wipf & Stock
An Imprint of Wipf and Stock Publishers
199 W. 8th Ave., Suite 3
Eugene, OR 97401

www.wipfandstock.com

PAPERBACK ISBN: 979-8-3852-1486-0
HARDCOVER ISBN: 979-8-3852-1487-7
EBOOK ISBN: 979-8-3852-1488-4

VERSION NUMBER 07/08/24

Scripture taken from the New King James Version. Copyright © 1982 by Thomas Nelson, Inc. Used by permission. All rights reserved.

All emphasis in quotations were added by the author unless otherwise indicated.

Contents

List of Figures | vii

Introduction | 1
1   The Character of God and Man | 19
2   Choices and Free Will | 24
3   The Potter's Freedom | 33
4   The Potter's Promise | 46
5   The Potter's Word | 64

Appendix 1: Response to Counterarguments | 89
Summary: Clearing Up Common Misunderstandings of Calvinism | 105
Appendix 2: What Does the Bible Say? | 112
References | 143
Subject Index | 147
Scripture Index | 153

List of Figures

Figure 1. The order of good and evil in the Calvinist and Arminian systems | 13

Figure 2. Arminian ballot. Image from *Modern Reformation*, May/June 1992 (https://image.isu.pub/200831202551-ce9dce80d74228ce9e21eb-30f585e16e/jpg/page_1_thumb_large.jpg) | 14

Figure 3. King David instructing Joab to number the people. Copyright: ClipART Educational Technology Clearinghouse (https://etc.usf.edu/clipart/67600/67661/67661_israel_nmbrd.htm) | 54

Figure 4. Micaiah before King Ahab and King Jehoshaphat. Image from iStock by Getty Images (Illustration ID 185057563) | 56

Figure 5. Job suffers. Image from iStock by Getty Images (Illustration ID 469199900) | 57

Figure 6. Judas realizing his sin. Image from iStock by Getty Images (Illustration ID 1370530483) | 62

Figure 7. The *ordo salutis* according to Arminianism and Calvinism | 74

Figure 8. Balance and imbalance between God's immanence and transcendence in the Arminian, Calvinist, and hyper-Calvinist systems | 107

Introduction

Dr. Leighton Flowers is the director of Evangelism and Apologetics for Texas Baptists, and leads the Soteriology 101 ministry, dedicated to opposing Calvinism. His YouTube channel has 73,900 subscribers and 941 videos. The channel's description says, "Former Calvinistic professor explains why Calvinism is not Biblical," raising this question: if it wants to refute Calvinism, what does it offer instead? He came out with a book titled *The Potter's Promise: A Biblical defense of Traditional Soteriology*, published by Trinity Academic Press. The book is obviously a critique of a referenced book by the well-known Calvinist apologist James White, with the title *The Potter's Freedom*.

Leighton Flowers's ministry has gained traction recently and is reaching many people. Thus, it would be worth addressing his criticisms of Calvinism, which we wish to undertake in the present book. This is all the more important, since with his book and his ministry, Flowers is leading many people away from orthodox Christianity, with his own departure from Calvinism setting an example.

Who Is Really the Traditionalist?

Leighton Flowers calls his brand of soteriology "traditionalism." Traditionalism, from Flowers's point of view, teaches that Christ loves every single person so much that he died for them all, and that God predestines every individual who is "marked in Christ" through faith to be saved. According to this view, it is each person's responsibility to humble themselves

A Critique of Provisionism

and trust Christ in faith.[1] With this, however, Flowers affirms the standard Arminian creed that man must choose Christ by practicing faith towards God's promises of salvation to all men. However, this leads him to all of the historical errors that have been spawned by Arminianism.

The name "traditionalist" may throw the reader off, as Flowers uses this term in contradistinction with the Calvinist system of soteriology. The "traditionalist" view is not connected in any way to the traditional view of soteriology that the mainline church has always proclaimed.

The Holy Spirit actively teaches the church throughout the ages, ever since the garden of Eden. Jesus says this: "However, when He, the Spirit of truth, has come, He will guide you into all truth" (John 16:13). This means that the Holy Spirit has revealed divine truth to the early church, starting at Pentecost all the way until the modern day. His teaching is uniform all throughout history. God never lies and neither does he change (Mal 3:6; Jas 1:17). "Jesus Christ is the same yesterday, today, and forever" (Heb 13:8). Paul also writes, "Therefore, brethren, stand fast and hold the traditions which you were taught, whether by word or our epistle." (2 Thess 2:15). Tradition in this sense is not the same as Roman Catholic tradition. It is simply the truth that has been handed down to us throughout the centuries, whether in written or spoken form.

Election is one of the Bible's most pervasive teachings. It is impossible to avoid. Even Pentecostals and Roman Catholics, such as Thomas Aquinas have recognized it. No matter what kind of theology a believer may have, he will have to come to grips with God's sovereignty and elective purposes. It would make sense that the early church was capable of discerning the truth in such an important doctrine such as election. In the Old Testament Israel was God's chosen people. This means that God has exclusively chosen only the nation of Israel with respect to salvation. No other nation was chosen on Earth. It was only starting in New Testament times that the different nations also shared in the salvation wrought by Jesus Christ. This sole argument would end the discussion on election. However, there are other issues raised in *The Potter's Promise* that must be discussed.

As such, who are we to bar God from choosing his own people in New Testament times, following the continuity of the Old and New Covenants? Flowers claims that the "Calvinistic" interpretations of Paul's writings do not appear until the fifth century with Augustine, and that the church fathers

---

1. Flowers, *Potter's Promise*, 9–10.

Introduction

exclusively taught libertarian free will.[2] This is false. In the New Testament, Paul wrote what Jesus taught, and later on, others such as Clement of Rome, Ignatius, Justin Martyr, Minutius Felix, Irenaeus, Clement of Alexandria, Tertullian, Origen of Alexandria, Cyprian, Novatianus, Athanasius, Hilarius Pictaviensis, Basil the Great, Cyril of Jerusalem, Gregorius Nazianzenus, Hilarius Diaconus, Ambrose, and Augustine all taught predestination from the first to the fifth centuries, all in close proximity to the time of Christ.[3]

The proponents of free will bring Clement of Rome[4] as an example of someone who espoused libertarian, autonomous free will.[5] However, just several church fathers have been known to change their opinions from time to time, such as Origen and Tertullian.[6] In AD 96, Clement of Rome (allegedly its first bishop) wrote the following in a letter to the Corinthian church: "Therefore He, being desirous that all his beloved ones should partake of repentance, *confirmed it by his almighty will.*"[7]

Ignatius was a bishop who was martyred in Rome. Before his death, he wrote letters to several churches, such as the one at Ephesus, in AD 110. He appears to have mixed views on election. For example, he writes, "Predestined before the ages for lasting and unchangeable glory forever, united and elect through genuine suffering by the will of the Father and of Jesus Christ our God," yet in the same letter, he also encourages the Ephesians to pray for nonbelievers, "that they may find God, for there is in them hope for repentance."[8] Also, to the Magnesian church, he writes that life in Christ "is not in us unless we voluntarily choose to die into his suffering."[9]

Polycarp was a contemporary of Ignatius, who wrote a letter to the Philippians in AD 110. In it he writes the following: "Knowing that by grace you have been saved, not because of works, but *by the will of God*

---

2. Flowers, *Potter's Promise*, 104–5.

3. Gill, *Cause of God*, 10–28.

4. This is likely the same Clement as spoken of by Paul in Phil 4:3: "And I urge you also, true companion, help these women who labored with me in the gospel, *with Clement also,* and the rest of my fellow workers, whose names *are* in the Book of Life."

5. Flowers, *Potter's Promise*, 140.

6. For example, Tertullian for a time fervently upheld the authority of Scripture. Yet later on in his life, he joined the Montanists, who claimed that the Holy Spirit spoke directly to the members of their sect, and that revelation was still continually being given to them. Tertullian later left the Montanists.

7. Gill, *Cause of God*, 11.

8. Gill, *Cause of God*, 11; Lightfoot and Harmer, *Apostolic Fathers*, 89.

9. Lightfoot and Harmer, *Apostolic Fathers*, 94.

through Jesus Christ" (1:3).[10] Polycarp is seemingly quoting Eph 2:8–10: *"For by grace you have been saved through faith, and that not of yourselves; it is the gift of God, not of works*, lest anyone should boast. For we are His workmanship, created in Christ Jesus for good works, which God prepared beforehand that we should walk in them." It is interesting to note here that verse 10 implies election, since God even foreordains our very works that we may walk in them; for this very work believers had been created since the beginning of time.

On the other hand, Polycarp did write other things that may seem to support free will in the same letter: "But the one who raised him from the dead will raise us also, if we do his will and follow his commandments and love the things he loved, while avoiding every kind of unrighteousness" (2:2).[11] Also: "If we please him in this present world, we will receive the world to come as well, inasmuch as he promised that he will raise us from the dead and that if we prove to be citizens worthy of him, we will also reign with him—if, that is, we continue to believe" (5:2).[12]

Other Arminians, such as Ken Wilson, claims that other Christin writings espoused free will. For example, the Epistle of Barnabas (written from AD 100–120) says, "Divine foreknowledge of human choices allowed the Jews to make choices and remain within God's plan, resulting in their own self-determination" (3:6).[13] However, when we look at the broader context, we read this: "So for this reason, brothers, he is very patient, when he foresaw how the people *he had prepared* in his Beloved would believe in all purity, revealed everything to us in advance" (6:3).[14] The fact is here that while it is true that God foresaw faith in some people, the reason these people believed is that they were prepared by God to have faith.

In other parts of the letter, the author also writes that "give very careful attention to our salvation, lest the evil one should cause some error to slip into our midst and thereby hurl us away from our life" (2:10).[15] He also writes the following: "If any desire to make their way to the designated place, let them be diligent with respect to their works" (19:1), and also "seeking out what the Lord seeks from you and then doing it, in order that

---

10. Lightfoot and Harmer, *Apostolic Fathers*, 123.
11. Lightfoot and Harmer, *Apostolic Fathers*, 124.
12. Lightfoot and Harmer, *Apostolic Fathers*, 125.
13. Wilson, *Foundation of Augustinian-Calvinism*, 20.
14. Lightfoot and Harmer, *Apostolic Fathers*, 164.
15. Lightfoot and Harmer, *Apostolic Fathers*, 164.

Introduction

you may be found in the day of judgment." (21:6).[16] From these last three references it may appear that the author puts a heavy emphasis on good works, even possibly to the point that a believer may lose his salvation, although this does not necessarily follow from his words.

Another example is when Wilson writes that in the Letter to Diognetus that "free will is implied in his capacity to become a 'new man'" (10:1–11:8).[17] Upon reading the actual source, this does not become apparent. However, the anonymous author of the letter also wrote this: "If you do not grieve this grace, you will understand what the Word has to say, through *whomever he chooses, whenever he wishes*" (11:7).[18] What this means is that the Word (Jesus) gives to us the words that we say to God in repentance and faith.

What should we make of these seemingly contradictory statements from these early church fathers, such as Ignatius, Polycarp, and the authors of the letters to Barnabas and Diognetus? Are they confused in their theology? Or are they flip-flopping like Origen or Tertullian? Instead, it could be that these early church fathers believed in a form of early concurrence, the Calvinist doctrine that upholds man's free will but also affirms God's electing people to salvation. Concurrence is reflected in Prov 16:1, which says, "The preparations of the heart belong to man, but the answer of the tongue is from the Lord." Concurrence will be covered in more detail in later parts of this book.

Justin Martyr described how salvation was prepared before prepared by the Father.[19] Irenaeus of Lyons wrote in AD 180, that God foreknew who would despise, and sun the light, and blind themselves yet more and more; because he determined to leave them to themselves, to their native blindness, darkness, and ignorance, with they love; and accordingly prepared regions of darkness, as a proper punishment for them.[20]

Later, as Pelagianism and Semi-Pelagianism gained ground, double predestination was defended by the martyr Gottschalk of Orbais in Germany in the ninth century. He rejected predestination based on God's mere foreknowledge, since this would make God's elective decrees contingent

---

16. Lightfoot and Harmer, *Apostolic Fathers*, 185, 187.
17. Wilson, *Foundation of Augustinian-Calvinism*, 21.
18. Lightfoot and Harmer, *Apostolic Fathers*, 304.
19. Gill, *Cause of God*, 12.
20. Gill, *Cause of God*, 15.

on man's will.[21] Gottschalk was the facilitator of a great debate about predestination in parts of Europe in the 840–50s, and even convinced several leading theologians of his time.[22] He wrote several works on predestination, including a shorter and a longer confession. For example, in his work *On Predestination*, Gottschalk writes:

> God, who does not know how to err nor can err, be deceived or deceive, never had to, has to, or will have to do anything—God forbid!—except how he once, simultaneously, and eternally has immutably arranged to carry out his foreknown, predestined, already fixed, already prepared, already determined, and already preordained gratuitous benefit of his grace over the elect and the just judgment of his justice over the reprobate, always according to the counsel of his will (Eph 1:11), showing mercy to whomever he wills with great goodness, and hardening, abandoning, and consequently condemning whomever he wills with no injustice, but certainly with high fairness, as befits a just judge, bestowing grace on the elect and rendering justice, judgment, and punishment to the reprobate.[23]

Before the Reformation and afterwards, predestination was rediscovered by theologians such as Wycliffe of England, Martin Luther, John Calvin, Theodore Beza, and propounded by later numerous theologians such as John Owens and the overwhelming majority of the Puritans. The acronym TULIP, which summarizes the five points of Calvinism, were merely refutations of remonstrant theology at the Council of Dordt. Remonstrant, Arminian theology itself was a reaction to Calvinist theology after it has taken hold in several European countries a time after the Reformation. Later Calvinist theologians include Charles Spurgeon, Jonathan Edwards, Charles Hodge, Herman Bavinck, Louis Berkhof, and in modern times R. C. Sproul and James White. Today, the Presbyterian and Reformed denominations are Calvinist. Other Protestant denominations, such as Baptists, Anglicans, and even Methodists have their Calvinist branches. It is worth noting that even Thomas Aquinas, who was the medieval architect of Romanist theology, believed in a form of predestination. For example, Aquinas describes the doctrine of predestination in eight articles in his well-known work *Summa Theologica*:

---

21. Berkhof, *History of Christian Doctrines*, 141.
22. Gumerlock, "Gottschalk of Orbais."
23. Genke and Gumerlock, *Gottschalk*, 57.

Introduction

> It is fitting that God should predestine men. For all things are subject to His providence, as was shown above (Question 22, Answer 2). Now it belongs to providence to direct things towards their end, as was also said (Question 22, Answers 1, 2). The end towards which created things are directed by God is twofold; one which exceeds all proportion and faculty of created nature; and this end is life eternal, that consists in seeing God which is above the nature of every creature, as shown above (Question 12, Answer 4). The other end, however, is proportionate to created nature, to which end created being can attain according to the power of its nature. Now if a thing cannot attain to something by the power of its nature, it must be directed thereto by another; thus, an arrow is directed by the archer towards a mark. Hence, properly speaking, a rational creature, capable of eternal life, is led towards it, directed, as it were, by God. The reason of that direction pre-exists in God; as in Him is the type of the order of all things towards an end, which we proved above to be providence. Now the type in the mind of the doer of something to be done, is a kind of pre-existence in him of the thing to be done. Hence the type of the aforesaid direction of a rational creature towards the end of life eternal is called predestination. For to destine, is to direct or send. Thus it is clear that predestination, as regards its objects, is a part of providence.[24]

It is interesting to note that the farther back in time we go, the more receptive the Roman Catholic church was towards predestination. Apparently, Flowers is moving in the same theological direction as Rome is today, away from predestination. Thomas Aquinas is more Calvinist than Flowers! This means that Calvinism is not a fringe ideology, but a serious system of theology that Christian theologians must grapple with.

This means that the term "Calvinist" soteriology is also somewhat inaccurate, since Calvin himself was not the only one who came up with the doctrine of election but followed a long list of Christian theologians in propounding this doctrine of the faith. Furthermore, Calvin was not the only Reformer during the sixteenth century who was rediscovering the doctrines of grace. Others, such as Luther, Zwingli, von Hutten, and Beza, came to similar conclusions around the same time, showing that they were all guided by the Holy Spirit. We could even rename Calvinism "Huttenism." It is only a name, just like Arminianism, Wesleyanism, or Pelagianism. The person who the doctrine is attached to is not important; only the doctrine

---

24. Aquinas, *Summa Theologica* I, Q 23, A 1.

is. It would make more sense to call Calvinism "traditional" soteriology! But in the rest of this book, we will stick to the name "Calvinist" theology because of widespread convention.

It also follows that any kind of teaching that stands in opposition to this "cloud of witnesses" (Heb 12:1) is very likely to be false, according to the saying "if it's new, it's not true, and if it's true, it's not new." When the Holy Spirit works in the church, most of God's people end up believing the same set of doctrines. Since Arminian freewill theology ultimately has its roots in Pelagianism of the fifth century, it follows that freewill theology is a theological innovation, not taught by Christ and the apostles or in the early church. Pelagianism was condemned at the Council of Carthage in 418, the condemnation later being ratified in the ecumenical council of Ephesus in 431. It was also subsequently condemned at the Second Council of Orange in 529.

There is nothing new under the sun (Eccl 1:9). Therefore, the roots of Flowers's "traditionalist" soteriology stands in opposition to orthodox soteriology. They may call themselves "traditionalists," but they follow another tradition, not the one found in the Bible. This is something Flowers's followers should keep in mind.

Manichaeism

Strangely, Flowers and other Arminian polemicists claim that Calvinism has partial roots in the ancient gnostic religion of Manichaeism. Is this really true? What is Manichaeism?

Mani (AD 216–74), a self-proclaimed prophet from the area which is now Iran, was the formulator of a syncretistic religion, combining elements from Christianity, Zoroastrianism, and Buddhism, and which influenced cultures as far apart was China and southeast Europe. Manichaeism had apparently reached Europe by the time of Augustine, who was at first influenced by it. A later form of Manichaeism called Bogomilism was reintroduced into the Balkans in the tenth century.

After Jesus' ascension into heaven, the twelve apostles had carried the gospel to countries far away from Israel. For example, according to certain accounts, Thomas brought the gospel to India and even China. Apparently, the area of Iran had also been reached by Christians and Jews. Mani himself had grown up in an Elchasaic Jewish community.

Mani came to reject the Jewish legalism inherent in the Elchasaic religion, and thus created a new religion, borrowing elements from the New

Introduction

Testament, Zoroastrianism, and Buddhism,[25] while rejecting the Jewish Old Testaments, except from certain parts, such as parts of the book of Genesis. Being a syncretistic religion, Mani greatly distorted the message of Christianity. While Mani believed in divine judgement, and practiced fasting, he also believed that he himself was the Paraclete, the Holy Spirit, and made himself the object of worship, because he believed that it was impossible for Jesus to have become man and to die and be resurrected. He said this, because he believed that the body and matter were inherently evil, whereas the soul originated from the realm of light and goodness.[26] Mani even gives the king of darkness the alternative name of "Matter."[27] The soul must be saved by knowing itself via inner illumination. In this way, the soul can share in the nature of God. This is completely contrary to Calvinism, which states that to know God is salvation.

But still, why do Arminian polemicists associate Calvinism with Manichaeism? In his writings, Mani describes five segments of his church community: doctors, ministers, administrators, and monks (who are much like priests), as well as the lay followers or hearers (auditors).[28] The first four groups consisted of the so-called "elect," and this is where the association between Calvinism and Manichaeism may possibly come from. However, we must keep in mind that correlation does not imply causation. Even though Calvinism and Manichaeism both use the term "elect," their meaning is entirely different. In Mani's system, the elect are merely members of the church hierarchy, whereas in the Calvinistic system, the elect constitutes God's people chosen for salvation. Interestingly, Tardieu, an author of a book on Manichaeism, concludes that Mani himself did not deny free will.[29] An auditor eventually becomes elect after a series of soul transmigrations. However, the auditor could also directly become a member of the elect.[30] This is not the same as election in the Calvinist system, since it is God who elects individuals for salvation and not man. People outside the religion could also become members of the Manichaean system, in effect destining themselves for becoming elect.

25. For example, Mani was given the name Buddha.
26. Stoyanov, *Other God*, 5.
27. Tardieu, *Manichaeism*, 82.
28. Tardieu, *Manichaeism*, 59.
29. Tardieu, *Manichaeism*, 37.
30. Tardieu, *Manichaeism*, 60.

A Critique of Provisionism

Islam is a religion that was based on Judaism and Christianity, albeit in a very distorted manner. For example, in the Qur'an Muhammed mentions Adam, the garden of Eden, Noah, Abraham, and Jesus. When reading the Koran, one gets the feeling that Muhammed merely copied large parts of the Bible. Islam believes in fate, which appears to be a distorted view of the Judeo-Christian doctrine of election. Thus, since Manichaeism is also a distorted version of the Christian religion, we can infer that election itself is a true and biblical doctrine, which was retained in Islam and Manichaeism, albeit in a distorted form. In fact, if the early church did hold to free will, we should expect to find distorted views of freewill theology in Islam. Instead, we find the opposite. To illustrate this even further, numerous pagan myths exist, which resemble the biblical accounts of creation, the fall into sin, the flood, and the Babel account in a more or less distorted fashion. This does not mean that these pagan legends are true, but they bear a kernel of truth in that they are based on real, historical events described the most accurately in the Bible.

One of the main characteristics of the Manichaean religion was the struggle between a good god, the androgynous Father of Greatness, and an evil god, the King of Darkness.[31] Among dualist worldviews, Manichaean Gnosticism is a form of absolute dualism, where the two principles, good and evil, are independent, coeternal principles.[32] The concept of dualistic gods of Manichaeism has its roots in Marcionism, which states that the god of the Old Testament is different from that of the New Testament. Here the devil is represented as God's eldest son, whereas later Bogomilism and Catharism claim that the devil forfeited his eldest sonship to Jesus when he rebelled against God.[33] The good god is responsible for all the good in the world, whereas the evil god is responsible for all bad things. The good god, being a spirit did not create the (evil) material world, rather the evil god is responsible for creation. This would make these two gods coequal in their struggle against one another. This is exactly the opposite of the God of Calvinism, since God is ultimately sovereign over all things. He is Almighty and All-Powerful, whereas the devil has only relative authority, and no absolute power whatsoever.

---

31. Flowers, *Potter's Promise*, 105; Frassetto, *Great Medieval Heretics*, 9, 23.
32. Stoyanov, *Other God*, 4.
33. Stoyanov, *Other God*, 161.

Introduction

Augustine

Flowers claims that Calvin based his views on predestination based on the teachings of Augustine, who himself based his views on Manichaean Gnosticism It may be true that Augustine held to Manichaeism at one point in his life, but he subsequently rejected it, and even wrote against the religion in works such as *De natura boni contra Manichaeos* and *Contra felicem Manichaeum*.[34]

Arminians and supporters of freewill theology oppose the teachings of the church father Augustine, who was one of the main formulators of the doctrine of election in the early centuries of the church. They claim that he influenced the Western church with his theology, and therefore that is why many churches today erroneously follow his views on election. This line of argumentation is very much like how Arians, such as Unitarians and Jehovah's Witnesses, argue, by trying to make their own minority view the mainstream.

Augustine also greatly influenced the Western church's concept of the Trinity. Augustine's teachings on the Trinity are accepted by Arminians and Calvinist alike. What Augustine added to the orthodox doctrine of the Trinity was the unity of the essence of the three persons in the Trinity. The three persons of the Trinity are said to "interdwell" one another (perichoresis). Augustine also formulated the teaching of the "filioque," accepted in the Western church, according to which the Holy Spirit was sent by both the Father and the Son, not just by the Father alone, as taught in the East.[35] Thus, they would be guilty of picking and choosing which one of Augustine's views they want to reject. Nevertheless, Augustine did admittedly have errant views on sacerdotalism and justification.[36] It is important to note that just as Calvinists do not blindly follow Calvin, neither do they follow Augustine blindly.

While it is true that Augustine did listen to the teachings of the Manichaeans, he rejected the sect's teachings after nine years. In his *Confessions*, Augustine describes how he long waited to listen to a Manichaean leader called Faustus, who was a skilled orator and proponent of Manichaean teachings. Augustine describes how he was disappointed when he was not allowed to ask Faustus questions that had perplexed him about

---

34. Augustine, *Confessions*, 77–79.
35. Berkhof, *History of Christian Doctrine*, 92.
36. Berkhof, *Systematic Theology*, 521.

A Critique of Provisionism

Manichaeism. After he was finally able to do so, he found Faustus to be ignorant of many things, such as the liberal arts. Augustine then lost all interest in Manichaeism. He describes his disappointment in the following way. Note how Augustine even refers to God's predestinating him in contrast with the errors of the Manichaeans:

> Lord my God, judge of my conscience, is my memory correct? Before you I lay my heart and memory. At that time you were dealing with me in your hidden secret providence, *and you were putting my shameful errors in my face (Psalm 49:21) so that I would see and hate them.*[37]

Furthermore, Augustine's earlier views on predestination involved God merely foreknowing who would believe in him. He later rejected this because he saw that such a view made salvation contingent on an element of free will within man.[38] Nevertheless, according to Augustine, God uses man's free will, meaning that he cannot be accused of being a determinist in the Islamic or Manichaean sense. In the *Enchiridion*, Augustine writes, "He used the very will of the creature which was working in opposition to the Creator's will as an instrument for carrying out His will, the supremely Good thus turning to good account even what is evil."[39] As B. B. Warfield writes on Augustine's role in the Pelagian controversy, it is not the faculty of man's will, but rather, man who has changed since the fall into sin. Grace does not make free will void, but rather acts through it and liberates it from its bondage to sin.[40]

In fact, it is not Calvinism that has its roots in Manichaean error, but rather, Arminianism has a stronger resemblance to this false religion. Arminians claim that God is not the root of evil. But where does evil come from? If evil somehow does not originate from something good, then by necessity it must be eternal in nature exactly how Manichaeism depicts it. As such, if evil is independent of God, even coeternal with God, then it is out of God's control. Calvinism valiantly opposes this dark, horrific thought. The Bible contradicts the eternality of evil in Gen 1:31, which says, "Then God saw everything that He had made, and indeed it was very good. So the evening and the morning were the sixth day." This means that all evil arose after the sixth day of creation. Satan, his angels, and all evil arose after

---

37. Augustine, *Confessions*.
38. Berkhof, *History of Christian Doctrines*, 136.
39. Schaff, *Nicene and Post-Nicene Fathers*, 269.
40. Warfield, *Augustine and the Pelagian Controversy*, 96–97.

Introduction

this point in time. Thus, evil arose out of something that was good.[41] For an overview, see figure 1.

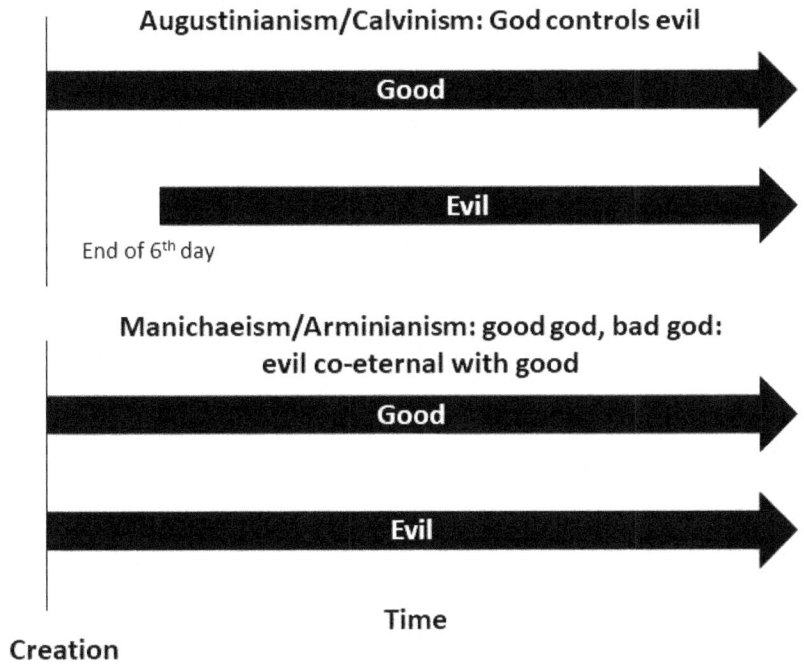

Figure 1

The Arminian affinity towards Manichaeism can be seen in some of the imagery it used to depict salvation. According to a popular American description of man's salvation, God has cast a vote for man, but Satan has cast a vote against him (figure 2). Therefore, man must exercise his libertarian free will and deliver the tie-breaking vote for or against God.[42] In free-will theology, God cannot control a moral agent such as man, which makes him less than omnipotent, and ultimately not sovereign. What is this if not the very picture of dualism where God needs man's help for him to win the battle against a foe of equal power and strength, the devil? Provisionists are the very ones who have a system of religion closer to the Manichaeism that they accuse Calvinists of!

---

41. Warfield, *Augustine and the Pelagian Controversy*, 76, 80.
42. Marsden, *Fundamentalism and American Culture*, 99–100.

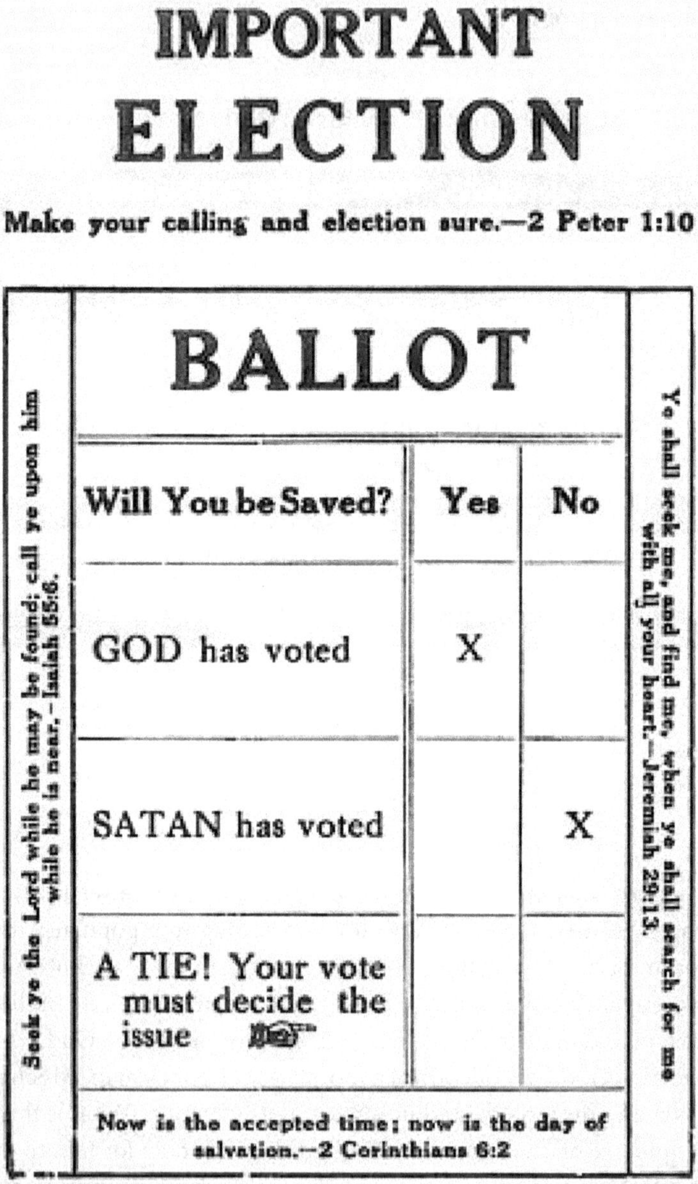

IMPORTANT ELECTION

Make your calling and election sure.—2 Peter 1:10

BALLOT		
Will You be Saved?	Yes	No
GOD has voted	X	
SATAN has voted		X
A TIE! Your vote must decide the issue		

Seek ye the Lord while he may be found; call ye upon him while he is near.—Isaiah 55:6.

Ye shall seek me, and find me, when ye shall search for me with all your heart.—Jeremiah 29:13.

Now is the accepted time; now is the day of salvation.—2 Corinthians 6:2

Figure 2

Introduction

Other Arminian polemicists believe in something called "divine self-limitation."[43] In other words, according to this theory, God is sovereign even over his own sovereignty. Olson cites Jack Cottrell as saying:

> God limits himself not only by creating a world as such, but also and even further by the *kind* [emphasis by Olson] of world he chose to create. That is, he chose to make a world that is *relatively independent* [emphasis by Olson] of him. . . . This means that God has created human beings as persons with an innate power to initiate actions. That is, man is free to act without his acts been predetermined by God and without the simultaneous and efficacious coactions of God. Ordinarily, man is allowed to exercise his power of free choice without interference, coercion or foreordination. By not intervening in their decisions unless his special purposes require it, God respects both the integrity of his own sovereign choice to make free creatures in the first place.[44]

This is meaningless. What does relative independence mean? Something either depends upon another thing or is independent of it altogether. Relative independence is independence nonetheless. If man exercises free will and initiates his own actions, then God is not sovereign over all, and thus loses this necessary divine attribute. How is God sovereign over his own sovereignty? God is free to do anything that he wants. The Arminian view by necessity elevates man and curtails God's freedom.

Calvin on Predestination

In an attempt to refute Calvinism from the very start, Flowers quotes Calvin allegedly describing the "dreadfulness" of his own teaching, as if trying to show that Calvin knowingly spreads harmful teachings. Following is the quote from Calvin's *Institutes*, book 3, chapter 23, paragraph 7: "I again ask how it is that the fall of Adam involves so many nations with their infant children in eternal death without remedy unless that it so seemed meet to God? Here the most loquacious tongues must be dumb. The decree, I admit, is, dreadful; and yet it is impossible to deny that God foreknow what the end of man was to be before he made him, and foreknew, because he had so ordained by his decree."[45]

43. Olson, *Against Calvinism*, 131.
44. Olson, *Against Calvinism*, 132.
45. Calvin, *Institutes*, 238.

A Critique of Provisionism

Flowers tries to make much of this quote from Calvin. True, God chooses men for salvation, but also for hell. As sovereign God, he has the right over every single creature in his universe. It is indeed dreadful for a man to be damned for his sins. But even the Bible describes God's judgments as terrible: "*For the day of the Lord is great and very terrible*; who can endure it?" (Joel 2:11) And Heb 10:31 says, "It is a fearful thing to fall into the hands of the living God." As to how man is also simultaneously responsible for his actions and is justly damned for his sins will be dealt with in a later chapter on concurrence. The Bible does describe dreadful things such as judgement and hell, and eternal torment. Jesus himself talked a lot about hell. But just because a doctrine talks about terrible things does not make the doctrine itself heretical, evil, or terrible.

Flowers tries to make it seem as if all of Calvinism can be summed up by God willfully predetermining some men to eternal damnation without them having a chance to do otherwise and tries to bring proof of this from Calvin's own writings. First, man cannot force God to give him a shot at salvation—Jesus never was forced to die on the cross. Jesus never had to take our sins upon himself. He did so by pure grace. God would have been perfectly justified in letting each and every single one of us perish in our sins. Furthermore, Jesus tells us that it is the most important thing, above all else, to "rejoice because your names are written in heaven." (Luke 10:20) We should remove the log from our own eyes and make sure that we are right with God before dealing with others.

Flowers shouldn't take Calvin out of context. Let's examine how Calvin really thought about election.

Calvin acknowledges that election is not the easiest subject in the Bible. But still, since it is in the Bible, we must not hide it, or think that it really isn't there. To do so would be to stifle God's blessings and the Holy Spirit, because God wants to teach us with this doctrine. Yet we must not pry with overt curiosity into this doctrine, lest we misunderstand something and become perplexed. Calvin says, "The secret things of God are not to be scrutinized, and that those which he has revealed are not to be overlooked."[46]

Rightly understood, election truly enriches the faith of the believer and humbles him before God:

> We shall never feel persuaded as we ought that our salvation flows from the free mercy of God as its fountain, until we are made acquainted with his eternal election, the grace of God being

---

46. Calvin, *Institutes*, 207.

Introduction

> illustrated by the contrast, viz., that he does not adopt all promiscuously to the hope of salvation, but gives to some what he denies to others. It is plain how greatly ignorance of this principle detracts from the glory of God, and impairs true humility. But though thus necessary to be known, Paul declares that it cannot be known unless God, throwing works entirely out of view, elect those whom he has predestined. His words are, "Even so then at this present time also, there is a remnant according to the election of grace. And if by grace, then it is no more of works: otherwise grace is no more grace. But if it be of works, then it is no more grace: otherwise work is no more work," (Rom 11: 5, 6). If to make it appear that our salvation flows entirely from the good mercy of God, we must be carried back to the origin of election, then those who would extinguish it, wickedly do as much as in them lies to obscure what they ought most loudly to extol, and pluck up humility by the very roots.[47]

Election truly humbles us. Salvation is completely of grace, of which election is the fountainhead. Election truly shows us that we can do literally absolutely nothing for our salvation. Those who are ignorant of election, or who would like to extinguish it, declare their own arrogance and pride. Nothing is due to our own merit or worth. All good things originate from God. Election ensures the salvation of individuals, thus assuring them of their unshakable salvation.

Why Does Calvinism matter?

Calvinism has uplifted many nations in Europe, as well as the United States and other countries. During the Revolutionary period in this country, the Presbyterian Church made major contributions for the independence of the United States. All of General Washington's colonels were Presbyterian, save one. In England, the saying went that the colonies had went after a Presbyterian minister, and that the War of Independence was a Presbyterian war. Calvinism made Switzerland one of the richest nations in Europe. Calvinism, and not any other Protestant religion, uplifted the Kingdom of Hungary to its golden age in the early seventeenth century, when the arts and sciences flourished.

The debate between Calvinism and free will affects so many facets of the Christian faith, most notably prayer, spiritual life, and missions. According to the saying, an earnestly praying Arminian is a Calvinist on his

---

47. Calvin, *Institutes*, 202–3.

A Critique of Provisionism

knees beseeching the Lord to open up their friend's or their family member's eyes to repent.

Calvinism strengthens missionary zeal. Almost all of the most notable missionaries of the eighteenth to nineteenth centuries were Calvinists. For example, it was William Carey, the very "father of modern missions," who took the gospel to India and translated the Bible into Hindi. David Livingstone is a well-known medical missionary who evangelized various African tribes. J. Hudson Taylor and Robert Morrison were the men who took the gospel to China. Taylor founded the China Inland Mission, which established five hundred schools in China and sent eight hundred missionaries to that country.[48]

---

48. González, *Story of Christianity*, 306–13.

1

The Character of God and Man

> "Just as He chose us in Him before the foundation of the world, that we should be holy and without blame before Him *in love*."
>
> (Ephesians 1:4)

ONE OF THE FOCAL points in the Calvinism-free-will debate pertains to the character of God. Here God's love and sovereignty are two of the most important points of discussion. Many of Calvinism's critics—Flowers included—portray the God of Calvinism as a cold, distantly removed, unloving God making cosmic decisions about human affairs without the input of the human beings that he created (although this description may reveal more of what Flowers himself thinks about God).

Flowers recounts how he started reflecting on the truths of Calvinism after listening to a song by a student praise band that used the words "take me, mold me, use me," and that started his journey out of Calvinism. Flowers then questioned God's prerogative in using his creatures for his own ends in the light of Christ's character.[1] But this is hardly understandable.

---

1. Flowers, *Potter's Promise*, 9–10.

A Critique of Provisionism

These are just two words in a single song. Songs are not infallible and can be changed.[2]

In contrast with John Piper, who asks, "How does a sovereign God express his love?" Flowers asks the question, "How does a loving God express His sovereignty?"[3] It is clear from this that for Flowers, love will dominate God's character as opposed to his sovereignty. But it is disingenuous and wrong for Flowers and like-minded Arminians to suggest that Calvinists have no inkling of God's love. Calvinists believe that God so loved his elect that he laid out his plans to save his people even before time. God orchestrates all historical events with the ultimate focus on finding and saving his people, even when they were mired in their sin and did not even know anything about God.

Flowers bases his characterization of God on extrabiblical emotionalism of what God ought to be like. For Flowers, it is incomprehensible to the human mind how God could elect some to salvation to show his love, and reprobate others to demonstrate his wrath and justice. Flowers's definition of God's love is imbalanced, emphasizing one of God's traits over the other. *God loves sovereignly.*

But yet, what does the Bible say about God's loving character? Ephesians 1:3–4 says,

> Blessed be the God and Father of our Lord Jesus Christ, who has blessed us with every spiritual blessing in the heavenly places in Christ, *just as He chose us in Him before the foundation of the world, that we should be holy and without blame before Him in love.*

Whether Flowers is content with this biblical definition of God's love or not, the Bible declares that election is good, biblical, and true. The goal of God's election is to choose a peculiar people for himself so that they may be holy, just as he himself is holy. To rescue men from their destructive sin, even though they don't deserve it, is a very loving action.

God loves all people, because he "makes His sun rise on the evil and on the good, and sends rain on the just and on the unjust" (Matt 5:45). Flowers responds to this Calvinistic argument by saying that that is nothing, because ultimately people will suffer in hell. But it truly is love, because

---

2. Indeed, some Arminian songs are also theologically incorrect. For example, the lyrics of the song "In the Garden" describe the joy that the singer has as he tarries in the garden with God no other has ever known, not even the giants of Christianity in the past two thousand years.

3. Flowers, *Potter's Promise*, 27.

God does not deal immediately with the reprobate by punishing them according to their sins, even though they fully deserve it.

But let's look at another biblical example of God's love. Judas was a son of perdition (John 17:12), and a devil, as Jesus himself said (John 6:70). Yet, Jesus truly loved Judas because he let him take part in his ministry. He loved even Judas, despite the fact that he later betrayed him.

Biblical Anthropology

To understand the character of God, it is important to understand how he relates to his creatures. Thus, it is important to understand biblical anthropology and the nature of man and sin. The weakest link in the Arminian thought system is its erroneous anthropology and its evaluation of the sinfulness of mankind. In contrast, the Calvinist system correctly describes the totally depraved condition of human nature and our innate inability to do anything good (Rom 3:12). The strength of the Calvinist system is that it is an experiential faith—an experimental faith, as the Puritans of old used to say. Calvinism is undeniable, because its truth claims are not mere abstract designs but *can be experienced*.

Flowers has a skewed view of God's love, based on his view of man. On page 26 of *The Potter's Promise*, Flowers writes:

> For example, we would be repulsed by someone who breeds puppies for the purpose of torturing any of them. Likewise, we would consider it evil for a father or mother to hate any of their children who they chose to conceive.[4]

This passage from *The Potter's Promise* shows how weak Flowers's anthropology is. It is quite unrealistic to compare murderers such as Adolf Hitler, Joseph Stalin, or Mao Zedong as mere frolicky, lovable puppy dogs. The Bible presents human sinfulness in a more serious way.

How does the Bible describe the totally depraved human condition? Let us read a description of the nature of man: "The heart is deceitful above all things, and desperately wicked; who can know it?" (Jer 17:9). The heart of man is incorrigibly wicked in its desperate struggle against the will of God. The depth of man's wickedness is unfathomable, it cannot be plumbed, it cannot be fully comprehended. We are more wicked than we would even admit to ourselves.

---

4. Flowers, *Potter's Promise*, 26.

A Critique of Provisionism

Man is so desperate in his wickedness that he even denies the obvious: the very fact that God exists, which is clearly attested to by the wonders of God's creation. Romans 1:20–21 says this: "For since the creation of the world His invisible attributes are clearly seen, being understood by the things that are made, even His eternal power and Godhead, so that they are without excuse, because, although they knew God, they did not glorify Him as God, nor were thankful, but became futile in their thoughts, and their foolish hearts were darkened." God exists, which is such a clear fact that makes atheism inexcusable. That is why atheists have been motivated to fabricate a godless cosmology, based on molecules-to-man-based evolutionary theory. Darwin himself described his theory as one long argument against God. Yet atheists suppress the truth of God's existence despite clear evidence from creation (Rom 1:21–23).

Then there is the example of how Pharaoh resisted freeing the Jewish people from slavery at Moses' behest. As we read through the ten plagues, we see how Pharaoh is wrestling in his heart: he wants to hang on to the Jewish people as much as possible, because they represent valuable slave labor to him. Yet at the same time God is prodding him to let go of his people by sending the ten plagues upon him. Despite the horror of locusts, frogs, and water turned into blood, Pharaoh still keeps a tight fist on the Jewish people and will not let them go. Such is the desperately wicked heart of man, who cherishes his autonomy and his own ways to the ways of the Lord, that even hard suffering will not change his mind. Multiple times in the book of Exodus we read that God hardened Pharaoh's heart (Exod 4:21; 7:3; 9:12; 10:1, 20, 27; 11:10; 14:4, 8; 17).

It finally took God to send the destroying angel of God to kill all the firstborns of Egypt for Pharaoh to finally let the Jewish people go. But even still after the Jewish people had left, Pharaoh still did not repent! He sent his army after the fleeing Jewish people to bring them back into Egypt. And that is when God finally put an end to Pharaoh's persecution of the Jewish people by drowning the Egyptian army in the Red Sea (Exod 14:27).

This kind of struggle also has a parallel in the book of Revelation. In Rev 9:13–21, we read about the four angels at the head of an army of two hundred million horsemen who were dispatched to kill a third of all mankind. This army caused horrific suffering on the inhabitants of the earth, but was not enough to convince the survivors of this terrible suffering to repent from their murders, sorceries, sexual immoralities, or thefts, or to stop them from worshiping their idols (Rev 9:20–21).

The Character of God and Man

Thus, we see that from a faulty view of man comes a faulty view of salvation in the provisionist system. Flowers's theology hinges upon the fact that man is somehow capable of responding to God's alleged universal love. Flowers is so fixated on this idea that one of his previous books (*God's Provision for All*) features a man pulling up another man by the hand on the book's cover. It could have come straight from the *Humanist Manifesto*.

But in fact, we see quite the opposite. Man is up in arms in rebellion against God (Ps 2). He has lost his way and does not even want to find his way back to God. As such, since nobody seeks God, he would rightfully send us all to hell. But despite universal rejection of God by all mankind, some are still saved. Because God so loved the world that he sent his Son Jesus to die for his elect. In this scenario, God literally has to choose some men from the mass of rebellious, lost mankind for salvation. It is the Calvinist system that makes more sense of man's condition than provisionism and makes for a far more consistent position, as we shall see in the upcoming chapters.

2

Choices and Free Will

"You did not choose Me, but I chose you and appointed you that you should go and bear fruit, and that your fruit should remain, that whatever you ask the Father in My name He may give you."

(John 15:16)

IN THIS BRIEF CHAPTER, Flowers brings Matt 22:1–14 as an alleged example of how men exercise their free will to choose God. This passage of Scripture describes the king of a land, who sends out invitations to his son's wedding feast via his servants to the inhabitants of the land. Twice he sends out his servants, but twice the invitation is ignored and rejected, and they even kill the king's servants. When the king hears of the misdeeds of the inhabitants of his country, he sends his armies and destroys the murderers. The king then sends his servants to invite all those who were on the highways, good and bad alike. And so, the wedding hall is filled with guests. Afterwards, a man is found at the wedding feast without a proper wedding garment. Since the man was without a wedding garment that all the other invited guests had on, he was bound and cast out into the outer darkness. The passage ends with verse 14, where Jesus says that "for many are called, but few are chosen."

Choices and Free Will

Flowers somehow tries to construe that the reason the invited guests come is because they freely accepted the invitation that the king had offered to them. At first blush, this may seem to be the case, but there is more going on that first meets the eye. Notice that Jesus did not say many are called, but only few accept the invitation. Few people are chosen. The guests must be chosen by God, not self-chosen, such as the man without the wedding garment who was cast out. Interestingly, the fact that there was such a man who came to the wedding feast refutes Flowers's claim. This one inconvenient fact overthrows Flowers's whole interpretation of Matt 22. This man seemingly wanted to come to the wedding feast, and thus apparently "accepted" the invitation. But he was still cast out despite his apparent "choice," meaning that salvation does not depend upon human will, rather on God's election. Many millions of people hear the gospel and repeat the sinner's prayer. Surely many, if not all take this prayer seriously and wish to claim salvation offered in the gospel. Yet so many people fall away afterwards and leave the faith. These are the seeds which fell on hard, rocky ground and may receive the word with joy, but endure only for a while (Matt 13:20–21). Saying a prayer is not the effective means of acquisitioning salvation, but the blood of Christ washing away the sins of a sinner.

Jesus says very clearly in John 15:16: "You did not choose Me, but I chose you and appointed you that you should go and bear fruit, and that your fruit should remain, that whatever you ask the Father in My name He may give you." This means that not only did Jesus choose some for salvation, he also appointed them to bear fruit. Proponents of free will may claim that Jesus was talking to his disciples only, but this is only a superfluous distinction. The first part of this verse refers to people choosing an individual Jesus. Unbelievers cannot produce fruit, since they are not in Christ, and there is no reason to suspect that what Jesus told those few disciples in John 15:16 cannot be extended to all who come to trust in him. In the same context, verse 19 says, "If you were of the world, the world would love its own. Yet because you are not of the world, but *I chose you out of the world*, therefore the world hates you." From this, it is clear that Jesus did not "choose the world" for salvation, but rather individuals. If Jesus did indeed choose the whole entire world, then everyone would be saved. This is the error of universalism.

In other words, the whole entire life of a believer has been delicately, precisely defined in such details that even our own good works have been predestined, not just our salvation. God is truly that gracious. We literally

A Critique of Provisionism

fully depend upon God's grace every step of our life and in every deed that we do! Ephesians 2:8–10 reflects this same sentiment: "For by grace you have been saved through faith, and that not of yourselves; it is the gift of God, not of works, lest anyone should boast. For we are His workmanship, *created in Christ Jesus for good works, which God prepared beforehand that we should walk in them.*" In the Old Testament, God tells Moses, "When you go back to Egypt, *see that you do all those wonders before Pharaoh which I have put in your hand*. But I will harden his heart, so that he will not let the people go" (Exod 4:21). Salvation is entirely outside of man. It is not dependent upon anything within a man, not anything that man thinks, wills, desires, or does. It is all God and nothing from the part of man.

John 3:8 says, "The wind blows where it wishes, and you hear the sound of it, but cannot tell where it comes from and where it goes. So is everyone who is born of the Spirit." We do not control the Spirit, rather he governs us. John 6:44 reiterates this sentiment: "No one can come to Me unless the Father who sent Me draws him; and I will raise him up at the last day." Clearly, salvation is not of man's will.

General and effectual call

In Reformed theology a distinction is made between the general call of salvation made to all men in general, and the effectual call, which is made only to the elect. The general call to all men is a bona fide, earnest call to repentance, just as Peter exhorted the Jews in Jerusalem to repent after the resurrection in Acts 2:28.

In Matt 13:3–9, Jesus tells the parable of the sower of the seed, who throws the seed unto four different types of ground. It appears that the sower is throwing the seed all over the field indiscriminately. One may think that this supports the Arminian viewpoint, since it seems that all men are called. It appears that no single special subset of "elect" people is specifically targeted by the sower. But is this really the case? Shouldn't the sower identify who the elect are, and give the gospel message only to these people?

The best way to evangelize is exactly the same way Jesus did in the Gospels. The fact that the call is also particularly addressed and made effectual to the elect can be seen from such verses as Matt 11:12–15 (see also Mark 4:9; Luke 8:8). When Jesus describes the receiving of the kingdom of heaven, he tells his listeners, "He who has ears to hear, let him hear!"

Choices and Free Will

In Matt 13:11 Jesus also says, "*Because it has been given to you to know the mysteries of the kingdom of heaven, but to them it has not been given.*"

Jesus preached his message repeatedly in this fashion. In Mark 4:23, Jesus says, "If anyone has ears to hear, let them hear." (see also Luke 14:35). A similar sentiment can be read in Rev 2:7: "He who has an ear, let him hear what the Spirit says to the churches." This is then repeated to the other churches in 2:11, 17, 29; 3:6, 13, 22. In the Old Testament, Deut 30:6 says, "And *the Lord your God will circumcise your heart and the heart of your descendants*, to love the Lord your God with all your heart and with all your soul, that you may live." This means that God actively circumcises the hearts of the Jewish people to love God.

Other similar verses include Matt 19:11, which teaches that the gift of celibacy has been given to some, since not all can receive it: "All cannot accept this saying, but only those to whom it has been given." Indeed, the apostle John says in John 3:27: "A man can receive nothing unless it has been given to him from heaven." This underscores the fact that everything has been given to us by sheer grace: our talents, our mind, our will, our repentance, our faith. Literally everything. When Jesus is being sentenced and later executed, he tells the Jewish leaders, "You could have no power at all against Me unless it had been given you from above. Therefore, the one who delivered Me to you has the greater sin" (John 19:11).

The converse is also true: God gives people over to spiritual stupor and spiritual blindness in Rom 11:8: "As it is written: '*God gave them* a spirit of stupor, eyes that could not see and ears that could not hear, to this very day.'" This verse quotes Deut 29:4: "Yet the Lord has not given you a heart to perceive and eyes to see and ears to hear, to this very day." Apparently, God actively hardens people to the gospel, which is in line with the Calvinist doctrine of reprobation.

Some may object that with general calling God offers salvation to some who he never intended to save, since both elect and nonelect are called indiscriminately. This may seem to be an apparent difficulty, but we must keep in mind that in order for God to achieve his *decretive* will, God sometimes changes his *preceptive* will.[1] This is something Arminian scholars also accept. An example is found in Gen 22:1–19, where God orders Abraham to sacrifice his soon Isaac for him. Verse 1 says that this was a test of Abraham's faith, to see whether he would be obedient to God. God's

---

1. Berkhof, *Systematic Theology*, 462.

A Critique of Provisionism

purpose was to use Abraham to present a figure of the Father sacrificing the Son for the sake of the elect.

God simply uses the mouths of the pastors, preachers, evangelists, and Christian lay people to reach the elect. Romans 10:17 says, "So then faith comes by hearing, and hearing by the word of God." As humans, we do not have access to the Book of Life, which contains the names of all the elect. The best we can do is to preach the gospel to all, and the elect will respond. Second Corinthians 2:15 says, "For we are to God the fragrance of Christ among those who are being saved and among those who are perishing." In 4:3, we also read, "But even if our gospel is veiled, it is veiled to those who are perishing."

Others may object in the following way: is God not mocking the unbelievers in demanding something that they cannot do because they are not elect? This is the false thinking espoused by Pelagius and his followers in the fourth-century church, described earlier. God also demands men to be holy, just as he is, to reflect his character.[2] In 1 Pet 1:15–16 we read, "But as He who called you is holy, you also be holy in all your conduct, because it is written, 'Be holy, for I am holy.'" And in a parallel verse Jesus says, "Therefore you shall be perfect, just as your Father in heaven is perfect" (Matt 5:48). Yet we also know that no man can keep the law of God perfectly.

One last note is worth mentioning here: if salvation is truly contingent upon man's libertarian choice, then what about babies dying in the womb? What do we make of the tens of millions of abortions since Roe v. Wade in 1973? Or what about those who cannot intellectually comprehend the gospel? Since unborn babies cannot even hear the gospel preached to them, let alone understand it, they cannot even make a freewill choice for or against Jesus Christ. This means that according to the Arminian view, all unborn babies are lost, without any kind of chance afforded to them to save themselves. What love is this?

Some opponents of predestination, such as Amolo of Lyons, acknowledged that unborn babies are condemned because they could not avail themselves of the grace in Christ. In a letter written between 850 and 852, Amolo of Lyons writes the following to Gottschalk of Orbais: "Some are of course counted among the evil and those to be condemned, who could not be anything else, such as those newborn babies who died under the guilt of original sin, who could not be helped by the baptism of Christ."[3]

---

2. Berkhof, *Systematic Theology*, 463.
3. Genke and Gumerlock, *Gottschalk*, 192.

Choices and Free Will

Proponents of freewill theology sometimes respond in the following way to salvage their theology by saying that God saves the unborn because they have not yet reached the age of accountability.[4] However, this is going well beyond the pale of Scripture and denies the exclusivity of the gospel. Furthermore, if infants are sinless until a certain age, this implies that original sin does not exist, and that the sinful nature is not passed on through the generations. This is full-blown Pelagianism: denial of original sin.[5]

In contrast, the Westminster Confession states the following:

> *Elect infants, dying in infancy, are regenerated and saved by Christ through the Spirit, who worketh when, and where, and how He pleaseth. So also are all other elect persons who are incapable of being outwardly called by the ministry of the Word.*[6]

In contrast, in the Calvinist system, God can do anything out of love. He can save infants even in the womb. As to how this happens, we do not know, but we should not force God into a logical box that is defined by our own understanding.

To keep their theology intact, Arminians must create a new, separate gospel for the unborn. In John 14:6, Jesus says, "I am the way, the truth, and the life. No one comes to the Father except through Me." Jesus is *the* way, not *a* way. This is the one and only single way to heaven. In heaven nobody can make the claim that they got there because they had not reached the age of accountability.

Other Arminians might respond by saying that God is just and will take all unborn babies to be with him in heaven. This merely leads to another conundrum: if God is just with the unborn, then he must also be just with adults as well who are in possession of their mental faculties. This means that God would have to judge all of us for all of our sins. This means that though unborn babies may go to heaven, adults all go to hell because Arminian theology has now switched the basis of salvation from Christ's exclusive sacrifice to justice. But even in this, the Arminian position contradicts the Bible. Psalm 51:5 says, "Behold, I was brought forth in iniquity,

---

4. This is something taught in Roman Catholic theology. According to the Catholic Encyclopedia, "The name given to that period of human life at which persons are deemed to begin to be morally responsible. This, as a rule, happens at the age of seven, or thereabouts, though the use of reason requisite for moral discernment may come before, or may be delayed until notably after, that time." Delany, "Age of Reason."

5. Sproul, *Willing to Believe*, 60; Steele et al., *Five Points*, 211.

6. Smith, *Systematic Theology*, 49.

and in sin my mother conceived me." Even babies are tainted with original sin since they were born into it through Adam and Eve. If God were to take these babies into heaven, he would be unjust by doing so, and would be letting babies into heaven despite their inherent sinful nature.

If election is conditional, there will always be those who cannot meet the specified condition. To meet any specific condition for salvation demands some sort of performance on our part, be it ever so little. This makes all the difference in the world. In this sense, Arminianism is truly semi-Pelagian in that a human factor is calculated into the plan of salvation, and it is different from grace-plus-works-based Roman Catholicism *only in degree*, whereas the Calvinist gospel is different in *kind*. This makes Arminian freewill theology a "Jesus plus" religion: Jesus may have died for sinners, but a human response necessary to ultimately seal the deal. This is so even in Wesleyan Arminianism, since prevenient grace gives way to cooperative grace to be effective.[7] Ephesians 2:8 says otherwise: "For by grace you have been saved through faith, *and that not of yourselves*; it is the gift of God."

How Does Human Will Work?

At this point it would be proper to describe how the will of man operates. One cannot isolate man's volition from other components of man's essence. Man's intellect, will, and emotion all constitute man's nature. They are bound up with one another, influencing one another. However, Arminianism isolates man's will from his other components. In the Arminian system, man is an independent actor, with an indeterminate free will, which he can exercise uninfluenced and uncoerced by any kind of external or internal factors.[8] But this way, man's choices are mere random events, like dropping a ball on the very top of the roof of a house, with the ball landing randomly on one side of the roof or the other. Man's choice become meaningless if not guided by some moral compass: *ex nihilo nihil fit*—out of nothing, nothing follows.[9] If there is no rhyme to man's will, then there is also no reason to it either, and man is reduced to the level of a brute, and man is not even responsible for his own choices, because they are not even his own.[10] Interestingly, a great champion of Arminian theology, Roger Olson himself admits

---

7. Olson, *Arminian Theology*, 36–37.
8. Smith, *Systematic Theology*, 325–26.
9. Sproul, *Chosen by God*, 51–52.
10. Hodge, *Systematic Theology*, 296–98.

this fallacy and says that the will is influenced and situated in a context, yet attempts to retain human autonomy in decision-making.[11] This cannot be: either God or man determines salvation.

Interestingly, at a physiological level, it seems that our decisions are not made by our conscious free will, but rather by some other component of our psyche. Benjamin Libet (1916–2007), a physiology professor at the University of California at Davis, ran several experiments where he had his experimental subjects perform some simple tasks (i.e., moving a finger or pressing a button) while sitting in front of a timer. The subjects were asked to note the time on the timer before them when they first became cognizant of their wish to perform the task. On average, there was a two-hundred-millisecond (0.2 seconds) delay between the time when the experimental participants became aware of their desire to perform the task and when they actually performed the task itself, with a margin of error of about fifty milliseconds. Libet also had an EEG device hooked up to the participants, and surprisingly measured brain activity initiating the act itself five hundred milliseconds before the task was actually carried out. This means that the participants' brain was actually preparing to perform the task three hundred milliseconds *before* the participants actually realized their will to perform the task.[12] Apparently, our choices are not determined by our conscious free will.

As we can see, the Arminian doctrine of free will runs into a dead end. Man's will is not free in an indeterminate sense. As Calvinist apologist James White admonishes Arminian scholars, they should consider that their theology wishes to restrict God's freedom by upholding man's freedom in choosing.

But how does man's will really work? As stated earlier, man's will works together with his emotions and his intellect. Man's free choices are defined by his *nature*. Man's responsibility is grounded in his ability to do certain things. As Arthur Pink describes it, man has the natural ability to do good, so thus he is accountable for believing or not believing. Yet at the same time, since he is dead in sin, he lacks the moral ability to repent and keep God' law.[13]

Proverbs 4:23 tells us to "keep your heart with all diligence, for out of it spring the issues of life." Jesus warns us in Mark 7:21 that "for from

---

11. Olson, *Arminian Theology*, 75.
12. Libet, *Mind Time*; see Kurzweil, *How to Create a Mind*, 229–30.
13. Pink, *Sovereignty of God*, 153–54.

A Critique of Provisionism

within, out of the heart of men, proceed evil thoughts, adulteries, fornications, murders, thefts, covetousness, wickedness, deceit, lewdness, an evil eye, blasphemy, pride, foolishness." Clearly, our desires and motives influence our mind, which in turn affect our will.[14] God, who is the author of freedom, by nature cannot sin. Neither can the redeemed, once in heaven sin, who have received a new nature. Adam, who truly had free will in Eden, still chose to rebel against God. Schaff comments about Adam's fall: "The fall of Adam appears all the greater, and the more worthy of punishment, if we consider, first the height he occupied, the divine image in which he was created; then, the simplicity of the commandment, and the ease of obeying it, in the abundance of all manner of fruits in paradise; and finally, the sanction of the most terrible punishment from his Creator and greatest Benefactor."[15]

How can sinners then choose Christ by their fallen natures? Romans 3:11 says that "there is none who understands; there is none who seeks after God." Man's will can do nothing to save himself, as Rom 9:16 says. Rather, God's people must be made willing in the day of his power (Ps 110:3). Jesus alone can set us free, not our own will: "*Therefore if the Son makes you free, you shall be free indeed*" (John 8:36).[16]

---

14. Pink, *Sovereignty of God*, 134.
15. Sproul, *Willing to Believe*, 54–55.
16. Pink, *Sovereignty of God*, 136–38.

3

The Potter's Freedom

"In Him also we have obtained an inheritance, being predestined according to the purpose of Him who works all things according to the counsel of His will."

(Ephesians 1:11)

This chapter deals with the sovereignty of God, and to what extent God is active in the life and activities of his creatures. It appears from this chapter of *The Potter's Freedom* that Flowers is more interested in giving as much "autonomy" and "libertarian freedom" to man as possible. He characterizes the God of Calvinism as a fatalist, controlling each and every single movement of the creature, playing them as puppets on his hand. Flowers sets this picture of God over against a kind of God who freely interacts with his creatures. He defines sovereignty as the temporal outworking of God's eternal omnipotence.

To illustrate this, Flowers uses the analogy of two different kinds of chess players. The first one is an old lady, playing both sides of the chess game by herself to ensure victory—thus allegedly the Calvinist God, who is sovereign over all movement within the world, even predetermining what the chess opponent would move. Over and against this comparison Flowers

A Critique of Provisionism

presents the traditionalist God as a wise and superior chess champion soundly defeating all of his opponents who come to do battle with him on the chessboard.[1]

However, both analogies break down, because they are unbiblical or do not portray the full picture. In Flowers's comparison, the chess champion wins all his matches by his skill and wisdom. However, in the real world, many, many people reject Christ. Does this mean that God, portrayed by the chess champion, has lost the great majority of his games? This seems to be the logical conclusion. Flowers's chess analogy makes no sense. God is not a loser, especially not to Satan. One of the meanings of Jesus's name means victory. It may seem that God has a purpose in giving people over to their sins in reprobation.

Furthermore, Flowers's analogy of the wise chess champion resembles open theism. According to this view, God makes decisions only after history begins, on the fly. This view clearly contradicts the many Bible verses which state that God predetermines everything (Prov 16:33; Acts 4:27–28; Eph 1:11).

The Bible clearly states that God is sovereign over every motion that happens during history. Ephesians 1:11 says, "In Him also we have obtained an inheritance, being predestined according to the purpose of Him who works all things according to the counsel of His will." Psalm 135:6 also says, "Whatever the Lord pleases He does, in heaven and in earth, in the seas and in all deep places." Sovereignty is a necessary attribute of God. There is nothing that is outside God's control. If there were, then that would mean God is no longer God, and this would lead to atheism.[2] If Flowers were consistent, why not allow as much "libertarian freedom" to man as possible, if that is what the definition is of a truly loving God? This would either elevate man to God's level, or vice versa, bringing God down to man's level.

Nowhere does Calvinism deny the freedom of secondary causes. Chapter 3, paragraph 1 of the Westminster Confession says this about the liberty of man:

> God from all eternity did, by the most wise and holy counsel of his own will, freely and unchangeably ordain whatsoever comes to pass; yet so as thereby neither is God the author of sin, *nor is*

---

1. Flowers, *Potter's Promise*, 36–37.
2. Owen, *Display*.

> *violence offered to the will of the creatures, nor is the liberty or contingency of second causes taken away, but rather established.*[3]

Chapter 20, paragraph 1 says this:

> The liberty which Christ hath purchased for believers under the gospel consists in their freedom from the guilt of sin, the condemning wrath of God, the curse of the moral law; and in their being delivered from this present evil world, bondage to Satan, and dominion of sin, from the evil of afflictions, the sting of death, the victory of the grave, and everlasting damnation; *as also in their free access to God, and their yielding obedience unto him, not out of slavish fear, but a child-like love and willing mind.*[4]

Calvinism is not the fatalism of Islam, where God moves humans like pawns on a chess board. In this view, man has no responsibility for his actions whatsoever and becomes totally passive.[5] As opposed to this, man is free, but his actions are also necessary. How are they necessary? Because they are determined and defined by his nature. Man's free actions are a self-expression of his own nature. Charles Hodge describes man's freedom this way:

> His volitions are truly and properly his own, determined by nothing out of himself but proceeding from his own views, feelings, and immanent dispositions, so that they are the real, intelligent, and conscious expression of his character, or of what is in his mind.[6]

Flowers's analogy of the wise chess master is also flawed. In his analogy, the chess master beats all of his opponents who come to challenge him. Obviously, in the analogy, God is the chess master who employs masterful arguments to convince all men to choose him for salvation. Is Flowers really serious about employing this analogy? If we look at the logical consequences of Flowers's analogy, it means that all men are saved. All men end up choosing God. Even the likes of Hitler, Stalin, and Mao.

In reality, the great majority of people end up rejecting God. Does this mean that these people actually beat the divine elderly chess master? How

---

3. Smith, *Systematic Theology*, 19.
4. Smith, *Systematic Theology*, 104.
5. I once had a discussion about the spread of liberalism in modern society with a Turkish friend of mine. A Muslim, he was resigned to the eventual spread of liberalism all across the country as if unstoppable.
6. Hodge, *Systematic Theology*, 285.

impossible! Flowers realizes that God is truly sovereign, and all-powerful. Thus, He has the capability of drawing to himself anyone who comes across his path via a spiritual chess match. In freewill theology, this means that God can persuade anyone to choose him. But since we know God can save anyone he chooses, and since we know that not everyone is saved, this can only mean that God wanted to save only a subset of humankind: the elect. Using the chess analogy, since the chess master beats anyone who plays him, this can only mean that only a small subset of chess players actually played against the chess master. The rest of humanity was simply disinterested in playing chess at all with the chess master. In reality, what this means is that people do not know God, and are alienated from him, and simply do not care to retain God in their knowledge. Romans 1:21 says, "Because, although they knew God, they did not glorify Him as God, nor were thankful, but became futile in their thoughts, and their foolish hearts were darkened."

Sovereignty and Omnipotence

Flowers's purpose with the chess analogy was to compare and contrast God's sovereignty with his omnipotence. Flowers's main point is that God is always omnipotent and defines his sovereignty in light of his omnipotence. In other words, Flowers's God is sovereign to the degree that he chooses in relation to his created world. God's infinite and mysterious ways accomplish his purposes in, through and despite the libertarian free will he has given to his creatures.[7]

In effect, Flowers lessens God's sovereignty. This is because man can surprise God by exercising his libertarian free will. In Arminianism, God always has to replan everything. Flowers even reinterprets verses 3 and 16 of Psalm 115: "Our God is in the heavens; he does all that he pleases [verse 3].... The heavens are the Lord's heavens, but the earth he has given to the children of man [verse 16]." Flowers reinterprets these verses to fit his provisionist thinking. This is eisegesis. Psalm 115 is talking about God who created everything and has a special relation with his people, Israel.

Verse 16 merely states that God created the earth as a dwelling place for man. It does not say that God ceded this portion of the universe to mankind for them to use it as we see fit. Since God created everything, he also owns everything. Man is not autonomous; he is merely a steward

---

7. Flowers, *Potter's Promise*, 36–37.

over God's creation, that's all what this verse is talking about. Man only has *temporary, relative authority* over the earth as its steward. This is what the "powers above" and the "rulers of the earth" mean in Isa 24:21, cited by Flowers. These are the rulers, authorities, cosmic powers, and "spiritual forces of evil in heavenly places" in Eph 6:12, the "evil powers of this world" in Col 2:20, and the spiritual rulers, powers, and authorities in 1 Cor 15:24 cited by Flowers.

If Flowers assigns man *absolute* autonomous control over his own domain, he is in effect making man into a demigod. Furthermore, the previously mentioned four verses also mention spiritual forces of evil and evil powers in heavenly places. Not only man but Satan and the demons would be loosed from under God's control! This leads to a dualistic system of religion.

Foreknowledge

The question of foreknowledge comes into question as a part of God's sovereignty. Flowers asks, "What do we know of the eternal dimension or the knowledge contained therein? How do we measure God's infinite ways and dogmatically assume a causal link between what is known in eternity and what happens temporally? Does God know it because He determines it, or does He determine it because He knows it? Or maybe He permits others to make determinations separately (autonomously)? When speaking of God, why is the term 'foreknowledge' even employed by the inspired biblical authors if a more applicable term like 'predetermine' is available and better suited? If He determines all things that come to pass, then what purpose is there in speaking of His mere knowledge or permitting of anything?"[8]

One must wonder, how could Flowers even ask such questions, based on his own provisionist views? If man is granted by God autonomous free will, then God determining anything is pointless. If there is no causal link between God's knowledge in eternity and temporal events in the created world, here and now, then it means that God is not in control. God is no God, and this leads to atheism. If man ultimately decides his own destiny, in an autonomous manner, then not even God can know man's decision, neither in eternity, nor any other place. Such a universe would quickly fall apart.

If man has autonomous free will to decide for or against God, then this means that men decide how populous heaven is going to be. But let's

---

8. Flowers, *Potter's Promise*, 40.

A Critique of Provisionism

look at John 14:2–3: *"In My Father's house are many mansions; if it were not so, I would have told you. I go to prepare a place for you. And if I go and prepare a place for you, I will come again and receive you to Myself; that where I am, there you may be also."* These verses tell us that Jesus is going to prepare a place for all those who believe in him. In another verse, Jesus says this to his disciples: "But to sit on My right hand and on My left is not Mine to give, but it is for those *for whom it is prepared* by My Father" (Matt 20:23). Note here that to sit at the right or the left of the Father was prepared for people, not because of any one thing they did.[9]

But how does Jesus know how the exact number of mansions to build beforehand if men decide whether or not they want to live in them? If provisionist thinking is correct, it might just be that Jesus built either too many or too few mansions for those who end up in heaven because they chose him. No, Jesus knows exactly how many mansions he is going to build, because he knows each inhabitant by name, precisely because he personally chose each inhabitant by name.

Why do the inspired biblical authors use the word "foreknowledge" instead of a more applicable term, such as "predetermine"? That is simply the word that they used. Instead of asking such questions, Flowers himself has to demonstrate that the usage of the word "foreknowledge" never means that God also predetermined everything. Note that Flowers also diminishes God's greatness by taking away his prerogative to determine all things and allows him only mere foreknowledge. Ephesians 1:11 clearly contradicts Flowers's provisionist philosophy: "In Him also we have obtained an inheritance, *being predestined according to the purpose of Him who works all things according to the counsel of His will."* God is not a passive God, recording events as they happen, blow by blow, reacting to man's choices. God is an active God, who proactively works out all events, precisely because he predestined them all.

What is also unsettling about Flowers's provisionist God is that for him, the past, present, and future both remain certain but also changeable. Does this mean that God can at some point in the future renege his promise to save us? Or to undo the cross? That he can send everyone to hell who has made it to heaven? After all, we are sinners and we deserve hell. Such a prospect is downright chilling in Flowers's world. But Heb 13:8 speaks differently: "Jesus Christ is the same yesterday, today, and forever." Flowers philosophizes that God is also so creative that he can accommodate change.

---

9. Genke and Gumerlock, *Gottschalk*, 143.

But just because God can possibly do anything doesn't mean he does everything we imagine. Flowers may not be impressed about such a God who predetermines all things, and thus is in total control, but Flowers's approval or disapproval does not determine biblical truth. And on the other hand, If God is unprepared, this does not evoke much trust, especially when he can change everything at a whim, like the capricious Allah of Islam.[10]

A Powerful God

What is so attractive about a powerful, sovereign God who has control over all events in history? Here in America, during our relatively short history, we have had a sheltered life against the tumults of history as in other countries. The consumerist mentality is widespread in many people and being allowed to choose without someone else's opinion being forced upon us is second nature.

Things were different in other countries, such as the country of Hungary in Eastern Europe where my ancestors lived. Hungary was invaded by the Mongols in the middle of the thirteenth century. Several centuries afterwards the Turkish conquest started, lasting until the late seventeenth century. During this era there was a time when a large portion of the country was occupied by the Ottoman Empire. Then came the subjugation to Austria, two wars of independence, two world wars, and then Communism for forty years. It was during the latter part of these stormy centuries of Hungarian history that Reformed believers turned to an almighty, all powerful, sovereign God, knowing that he would save them from utter destruction. It was comforting for them to know that God was ultimately in control and was working all things for their good. Their only comfort in life being the fact that they are not their own, but belong with body and soul, both in life and in death to their faithful Savior Jesus Christ.[11] In the deepest hours of despair during the trials of Communism, Hungarian believers turned to God, hoping and knowing that God would save them from their enemies. And, in 1989 the Evil Empire[12] crumbled and fell . . . God is great. God is sovereign. "And He has made from one blood every nation of men to dwell

---

10. According to Surah 2:106 of the Qur'an, "if We ever abrogate a verse or cause it to be forgotten, we replace it with a better or similar one. Do you not know that Allah is Most Capable of everything?"
11. Heidelberg Catechism, question 1.
12. The former Soviet Union.

A Critique of Provisionism

on all the face of the earth, and *has determined their preappointed times and the boundaries of their dwellings."* (Acts 17:26). Only Calvinism offers this, not Flowers's provisionism.

The Doctrine of Concurrence

Man's responsibility and God's predestination go together. This is what mainstream Calvinism has always emphasized. This is called the doctrine of concurrence. Arminianism is imbalanced, since it overemphasizes man's responsibility. Hyper-Calvinism overemphasizes God's election. Such overemphasizing leads to imbalance and error. Flowers is targeting hyper-Calvinism, calling it true Calvinism, when in reality, this is not so.

Do the Scriptures really teach this doctrine? Let us examine some Bible verses that indeed teach concurrence.

In the Old Testament, several passages describe God and man working together. For example, Prov 16:1 says, "The preparations of the heart belong to man, but the answer of the tongue is from the Lord." Provisionists and Arminians falsely caricaturize the God of Calvinism as a puppet master, but in Prov 21:1, we read, "*The king's heart is in the hand of the Lord*, like the rivers of water; *He turns it wherever He wishes.*" The New Testament teaches the same concept: "Therefore, my beloved, as you have always obeyed, not as in my presence only, but now much more in my absence, work out your own salvation with fear and trembling; for it is God who works in you both to will and to do for His good pleasure" (Phil 2:12–13). In these verses we see how man prepares his heart, but because God is the one working in man. God directs the heart and mind of the king and in the will of man. And God also works in us salvation.

In contrast with Arminianism, God intervenes in the hearts and minds of men, directing their thoughts and actions according to his plan. Yet at the very same time, man is responsible for his actions. Paul exhorts his readers to work out their own salvation. Is this works-based salvation? No, it is not! Paul finishes his exhortation by saying that it is God himself working in man *both to will and to do* for God's own pleasure and purposes.

How can this be? How is it that God predestines and guides all actions? At this point man tries to peel away the veil and gaze into the deep mysteries of God. But it has not been given to man to understand such things. God's ways are higher than ours, and they are also incomprehensible to us. We cannot fully comprehend God. The doctrine of the Trinity states that God is Father, Son, and Holy Spirit, three persons in one Being. It is a mystery. Election and man's responsibility is also a mystery! Do Calvinists utilize the "mystery card" to explain away election at their own whim? No, simply because as we have seen previously, the Bible does talk about certain verses which appear to talk about man's responsibility: man is commanded to believe, to trust God, and to have faith and repent. For the Calvinist, this is all good and well. This is Christian teaching. But what cannot be ignored by Arminians are those sets of verses, which unequivocally present God's sovereign election. By choosing to ignore these verses, Arminians are in error and reject the authority of Scripture, as defined by the principle of *sola scriptura*. It is these verses, such as Prov 16:1, 21:1, and Phil 2:12–13, which bring God's election and man's responsibility together in a single statement.

To illustrate the biblical principle of concurrence, let us look at some examples. In Matt 27:3–4 we read this: "Then Judas, His betrayer, seeing that He had been condemned, was remorseful and brought back the thirty pieces of silver to the chief priests and elders, saying, '*I have sinned* by betraying innocent blood.'" Yet it is also true that Jesus was sacrificed by the Father as a part of his determined purpose and foreknowledge (Acts 2:22–23). This is a practical example of how man's will and God's will come together in one act. Judas was selfish and stole from the common purse of the apostles. He was looking out for only himself. Judas carried out his plan to betray Jesus for a mere thirty pieces of silver. It was his own plan, which he carried out irrespective of God's will. Yet at the same time it was an act which led to Jesus's condemnation by the Jewish chief priests, crucifixion and death at the hands of the Roman soldiers. These were all events orchestrated by God to ultimately bring about the salvation of men.

Another well-known example is that of Moses pleading with Pharaoh to let the Jewish people go. In the early chapters of the book of Exodus we read how a new Pharaoh came in Egypt who did not know Joseph, and who enslaved the Jewish people. Pharaoh did not want to let go of a multitude of people who could serve as manpower for all of his work projects. In Exod 4:21 we read, "And the Lord said to Moses, 'When you go back to Egypt, see that you do all those wonders before Pharaoh which I have put in your hand. But *I will harden his heart*, so that he will not let the people go.'" Two difficulties arise for freewill theology. First, why would God harden Pharaoh's heart so that he would *not* let God's people go? Is God working against himself? Or perhaps God has a higher motive for doing so? Second,

A Critique of Provisionism

if man truly has libertarian free will, just as provisionists claim, why is it that God hardens Pharaoh's heart to begin with?

If provisionism is true, the text should read: "I have foreseen that Pharaoh will harden his heart, so that he will not let the people go." Here from the outset, it is God who initially hardens Pharaoh's heart. As to why God will harden Pharaoh's heart, we find a clue in Exod 7:3: "And I will harden Pharaoh's heart, *and multiply My signs and My wonders in the land of Egypt.*" This verse suggests that the reason God will harden Pharaoh's heart is to display his power, to show that he indeed is mighty to save his people from the depths of slavery from the greatest tyrant that lived at that time and lead them to freedom to worship him as their God. Indeed, Exod 4:21 also mentions that God had foreordained that Moses would perform many wonders before Pharaoh that he had placed in Moses' own hand. The hardening of Pharaoh's heart and God's very course of action with Moses all show that all things regarding Pharaoh, Moses, and the freeing of the Jewish people have all been decreed beforehand by God.

Afterwards, in chapter 7 we read about how the Egyptian magicians were incapable of replicating all of Moses' and Aaron's wonders. In Exod 7:13 we read "And Pharaoh's heart grew hard, and he did not heed them, as the Lord had said." This verse seems to tell us that Pharaoh's heart grew hard by itself, as also in verses 14 and 22, and in Exod 8:19 and 9:7.

However, in the next chapter, when the frogs came up to plague the Egyptians we now read: "But when Pharaoh saw that there was relief, *he hardened his heart* and did not heed them, *as the Lord had said*" (Exod 8:15). Here it is now Pharaoh who is hardening his own heart, but just as the Lord had said beforehand, in Exod 4:21, because it was part of God's plan to harden Pharaoh to bring God glory by showing his power. Exod 8:32 again says, "But Pharaoh hardened his heart at this time also; neither would he let the people go." Again, God hardens Pharaoh's heart in Exod 9:12: "But the Lord hardened the heart of Pharaoh; and he did not heed them, just as the Lord had spoken to Moses."

As we can see here both God and Pharaoh are hardening Pharaoh's heart. This is a perfect example of concurrence. This episode portrays how both man and God are see-sawing back and forth. At one time Pharaoh hardens his own heart, at other times it is God who is doing this.

Also, there is something very telling about the state of Pharaoh's heart that shows that libertarian free will is not a factor in man's salvation. After the plague of hail in Exod 9:27–30 we read: "And Pharaoh sent and called for Moses and Aaron, and said to them, 'I have sinned this time. The Lord is righteous, and my people and I are wicked. Entreat the Lord, that there may be no more mighty thundering and hail, for it is enough. I will let you go, and you shall stay no longer.' So Moses said to him, 'As soon as I have gone out of the city, I will spread out my hands to the Lord; the thunder will cease, and there will be no more hail, that you may know that the earth is the Lord's. *But as for you and your servants, I know that you will not yet fear the Lord God.*'" Here it appears that Pharaoh is using the right words, he is even admitting his own sin and wickedness. It sounds like the beginning of the sinner's prayer by Campus Crusade for Christ. But why is Pharaoh "repenting"?

In 2 Cor 7:10 we read about godly sorrow, which leads to repentance and salvation, but worldly sorrow produces death. Pharaoh is sending away the Jewish people because they are causing a larger problem with the accompanying plagues than if he were to send them away. Pharaoh's heart is still hard, and Moses knows this. He tells this to Moses: he will not yet fear the Lord God, despite the terrible calamities that have befallen him and his people. Moses proceeds to tell Pharaoh that once he gets out of the city, the hail will cease. And truly, in verse 34 we read that once Moses had left the city and the hail had indeed ceased, Pharaoh hardened his heart yet again and sinned more and hardened his heart and did not let the children of Israel go. Apparently the "repentance" was only temporary. Once the hail stopped, Pharaoh had no more reason to repent anymore, and reverted to his former ways.

Just to drive it home, Pharaoh again undergoes a pseudo-repentance in Exod 10:16–18 when the eighth plague hits, with the locusts eating away whatever vegetation that the hail had left: "Then Pharaoh called for Moses and Aaron in haste, and said, 'I have sinned against the Lord your God and against you. Now therefore, please forgive my sin only this once, and entreat the Lord your God, that He may take away from me this death only.' So he went out from Pharaoh and entreated the Lord." But then verse 20 we read: "But the Lord hardened Pharaoh's heart, and he did not let the children of Israel go."

After the tenth plague, Pharaoh's kingdom lies in ruins. The animals have been killed, the vegetation has been destroyed, the plagues have come and gone and taken a very deep toll on the inhabitants of the land. The Egyptians' firstborn have also been killed. Even Pharaoh's own firstborn son lies dead in the royal palace. Any sane person would by now have let

A Critique of Provisionism

go of the Jewish people, because they are costing Pharaoh much more than what he can profit out of them. Yet in Exod 14:4 and 14:8 we read that even after the Jewish people had gotten up and left Egypt, Pharaoh's heart is hardened yet one last time. He rushes with his army of six hundred chosen chariots after the fleeing Jewish people who, with divine help, cross the Red Sea as if upon dry land, after which the waves close in on Pharaoh and his army, who meet their doom in the crashing waves.

The battle between God and Pharaoh displays vividly the struggle within man's heart against God. Man is so self-absorbed and desire so much to rule over his own life that it is impossible for him to repent and "turn his heart" over to the Lord as the proponents if freewill theology believe. Man's heart is so desperately wicked, who can know its depths (Jer 17:9)? Free will theology underestimates the sinfulness, the wickedness, and the level of depravity in man's heart. Man by nature cannot choose God, only himself. It takes divine intervention to reach in and turn man's heart of stone into a soft heart of flesh.

The next part of the Bible which illustrates concurrence are the three parables of faith and repentance in Luke 15. These three parables are about the lost sheep (verses 4–7), the lost coin (verses 8–10), and the prodigal son (verses 11–32). The first two parables illustrate how God takes the initiative in faith due to man's inability. First, we have the lost sheep, who has wandered away from the flock. Sheep are dumb animals, and they are incapable of finding their way back to the shepherd's house, even if they wanted to. It is thus incumbent upon the shepherd himself to go find the lost sheep and bring him back to the house. The second parable, that of the lost coin, depicts man even as an inanimate object, incapable of willing which way it would go. As an object without a mind of its own, the only thing it knows how to do is to roll away into some dark, dusty corner underneath the bed where it has to *passively wait* until it is found by the house owner. Here again both the coin and the sheep, representing the lost sinner, are passive in initiating salvation. Their willful decisions do not play any role in their being found.

However, the parable of the prodigal son is different, in that it describes the active role of faith in salvation. All three parables in Luke 15 fit together to show true faith from all angles. In verse 16 we have the prodigal son who has rejected his father's house and taken out his inheritance in advance and has used it as he saw fit to dispose of, living prodigally. A great famine has come in the land, and after having spent the last of his money, he is in want. He has to feed swine, but nobody gives him anything to eat. In verses 17–19 we read, "How many of my father's hired servants have bread enough and to spare, and I perish with hunger! I will arise and go to my father, and will say to him, 'Father, I have sinned against heaven and before you, and I am no longer worthy to be called your son. Make me like one of your hired servants.'" The prodigal son in his abject poverty and need finally comes to himself and sees the result of rejecting his father. He sees his sin and yes, he decides to arise and go back to his father. He even plans out a short speech to tell his father as a sign of his true, godly repentance.

As we see here, concurrence does involve both God's will and man's will. Both are true simultaneously in a mysterious way. They are both active at the same time and complement one another. Yet it is God who initiates salvation by reaching out to some who are lost in their sin. To do this, God himself has to choose whom he will save and choose whom he will not save. Calvinism presents the full story of faith, but provisionism presents only a half-way solution.

4

The Potter's Promise

"But as for you, you meant evil against me; but God meant it for good, in order to bring it about as it is this day, to save many people alive."

(Genesis 50:20)

Chapter four of Flowers's book starts with an expose of the so-called "messianic secret." In Mark 9:9, Matt 16:20, Mark 3:12, and Mark 8:30 Jesus strictly forbade his disciples to tell anyone about him. In other words, the Messiah's plan of redemption was kept under wraps for a time, to be revealed later in greater detail, at Pentecost. First Corinthians 2:7–8 gives us the reason why: "But we speak the wisdom of God in a mystery, *the hidden wisdom which God ordained before the ages for our glory, which none of the rulers of this age knew; for had they known, they would not have crucified the Lord of glory.*" Had the Jewish leaders and Pilate known who Jesus truly was, they would not have crucified him.[1]

But this way, they would have made Jesus' sacrifice on the cross null and void. According to worldly logic, Jesus should have showed himself publicly to the world so that as many people as possible would believe in him and be saved—a true manifestation of God's love, according to Flowers.

---

1. Flowers, *Potter's Promise*, 46–47.

In fact, Jesus' family members urge him to do so in John 7:2–5: "Now the Jews' Feast of Tabernacles was at hand. His brothers therefore said to Him, *'Depart from here and go into Judea, that Your disciples also may see the works that You are doing. For no one does anything in secret while he himself seeks to be known openly. If You do these things, show Yourself to the world.' For even His brothers did not believe in Him.*"

If Flowers's provisionism is true, and if God truly loves all people, and sent Christ to die for all those who choose him, then it should follow that Jesus should have proclaimed himself openly. But as the previously cited passage from Matt 7 says, this is an unbelieving viewpoint. It is not what the Bible teaches. While Jesus did keep his messianic identity secret for a time, until the cross, this is inconsistent with libertarian free will. But it is fully consistent with Calvinism.

The question is, did Jesus come to die for all people? Did he come to officiate a gospel awakening in Billy Graham–like style, preaching salvation to millions?

John 1:11 says, "He came to His own, *and His own did not receive Him.*" How could Jesus know who belonged to Him, had he not elected them beforehand? Interestingly, this verse also says that even His own chosen believers did not receive him but rejected him at first. What a contrast to the foreknowledge theory of provisionism. Obviously, Christ came to his own, whom he had elected from all eternity out of his mere good pleasure. At first, they rejected him, because of their total depraved nature, and so Christ had to open their mind and understanding so as to receive him. Matthew 20:28 also says, "Just as the Son of Man did not come to be served, but to serve, *and to give His life a ransom for many.*" A ransom for many, *not all.*

Let's take a look at another passage of Scripture in John 17:9: "I pray for them. *I do not pray for the world* but for those whom You have given Me, for they are Yours." Here, it is plainly stated that Jesus prays not for the universal salvation of all mankind, but for the elect only, whom he came to save. Jesus could not have come to die for the entire world, because had he done so, all would be saved. There is efficacy in the blood of Christ. Isaiah 55:11 says, "So shall My word be that goes forth from My mouth; it shall not return to Me void, but it shall accomplish what I please. *And it shall prosper in the thing for which I sent it.*" Jesus did not die in vain for the great majority of humankind. If God the Father can achieve salvation for his elect, and the Holy Spirit can regenerate and sanctify all who are saved, then surely Jesus saves all those who he died for. In other words, if God purchased his people with the blood of Christ, then he will receive every single one of the elect. God will not be shortchanged. He will not forfeit that which he purchased.

Judicial Hardening

Judicial hardening plays a role in our understanding of election and predestination. It makes perfect sense according to the Calvinist system in which God rejects the reprobate—while still maintaining their responsibility, and thus the reason why they can justly be damned. However, Flowers has to undergo mental gymnastics in order to accommodate it in his provisionist system. The fact that Flowers adapts it to his provisionist system means that he tacitly agrees with the biblical doctrine of reprobation.

Again, if God truly loved each and every single individual in the whole entire world that was ever born, it would make no sense for God to harden anyone's heart. By doing so, God distances the person from salvation. In provisionism, God should be doing anything and everything possible for the softening of men's hearts and the salvation of all. Otherwise, God is not truly powerful to save.

How is it that Isa 45:7 says this about God? "I form the light and create darkness, I make peace and create calamity, I, the Lord do all these things." Paradoxically, the Bible does say that God is good, yet calamities and disasters are also in his plan, but he is not the author of them. According to Piper, light is contrasted with darkness, peace with calamity. This is an example of a merism, which means that God is control of everything.[2] God is *so much in control*, that he forces evil to move only in the very confines that he dictates to it.

Many will object to ascribing evil to God. Roger Olson, a strong proponent of Arminianism, asks if the God of Calvinism is responsible for causing unbelievable suffering. In his book *Against Calvinism*, Olson describes how he was visiting a hospital one time and overheard the terrible screams of agony of a three-year-old child for half an hour. The child was possibly dying a slow, agonizing death. He then recounts the story of how a sex maniac abducted a young girl, took her to a forest where he raped her, strangled her to death, and threw her body into the river. Olson then asks,

---

2. Piper, *Providence*.

The Potter's Promise

where was God? Did the God of Calvinism really cause all this to happen?[3] Flowers also asks a similar question on page 54 of his book.

Arminians such as Flowers and Olson may think this is a crushing blow to the Calvinist viewpoint, but it is not. In fact, it is an indictment against Arminianism. How? We have to think about this in a wider context. If the Arminian position was true, and God did not let these bad, evil things to happen, then who is responsible for them? Who was the ultimate cause for these horrific events? The Arminians would point their finger to Satan: the devil did it, the epitome of all evil. But think what happens when absolute power is ascribed to Satan: this means that Satan can carry out his will in doing evil as an *independent, sovereign actor*. In the Arminian system God does not have control over Satan and cannot bind him. Arminians may object, by saying that their God is greater than Satan and can stop him, but how do they really know this? They are not omniscient to know this.

If Satan had the absolute power to carry out his wicked, malicious will, then every single child in every single medical ward would be screaming at the top of their lungs, suffering from indescribable pain. Tsunamis, tidal waves, and earthquakes would be crashing all over the globe. All the atomic bombs in the world would go off at once. In a word, all hell would break loose, if it were not for God's absolute sovereignly withholding hand. It is vitally important here to understand that God controls evil in such a way as to take it where he wants it to go, not where Satan wants it to go.

Fortunately, this does not happen, because God is sovereign and absolutely in control. Satan has absolutely *zero absolute power*. In fact, Satan has zero power to begin with, since he is only a created being. This should be a source of great encouragement to believers in their struggle against the world, sin, and the devil. This means that we do not have to fear the devil. In the Calvinist system, God sovereignly has all evil under his control and allows sin to go on for only so long. On the other hand, in Flower's provisionist system, God is powerless to stop this evil from going on, however loving he may be.

To understand the fact that the devil has no absolute power, but only relative, let us turn to what the Bible says about the power of the devil. In Luke 4:6, we read, "And the devil said to Him, 'All this authority I will give You, and their glory; *for this has been delivered to me*, and I give it to whomever I wish.'" God's power and authority is innate: it is properly his. This is because God is Creator and called all things into being. However, since

---

3. Olson, *Against Calvinism*, 89–90.

the devil is also a created being, he can only receive something that is not properly his. That is why this verse says that authority has been delivered to him. The devil did not create this authority. It is not properly his. Satan is only a mere tool.

So also the four beasts in the night vision of Dan 7 were also given dominion, such as the four-headed leopard (verse 6). In fact, the little horn of verse 21 *even makes war against the saints and prevails against them.* However, since their power is only temporary, their power is taken away from them by God whenever and wherever he decrees (verses 12, 26), and the court of God shall judge the little horn and condemn him (verse 26).

Let us look at what is the worst crime in history: the death of our Savior on the cross. Here the very Son of God was tortured, mocked, and died an excruciating death on a horrific torture tool of the Romans. Yet, according to Isa 53:10: "*Yet it pleased the Lord* to bruise Him; He has put Him to grief." Yet it pleased the Lord, because this most heinous of all sins caused the salvation of millions. God is truly in the business of turning evil into good (Gen 50:20).

In a similar vein, Luke 22:31 says this: "And the Lord said, 'Simon, Simon! Indeed, *Satan has asked for you,* that he may sift you as wheat.'" Here the Lord Jesus is warning Peter that temptation shall befall him, a test of his faith awaits at the hand of Satan, who has asked for him. Note here that Satan must humbly ask for Peter first from God; he cannot just rudely snatch Peter away without asking. Let us read Matt 16:21–23: "From that time Jesus began to show to His disciples that He must go to Jerusalem, and suffer many things from the elders and chief priests and scribes, and be killed, and be raised the third day. Then Peter took Him aside and began to rebuke Him, saying, 'Far be it from You, Lord; this shall not happen to You!' But He turned and said to Peter, '*Get behind Me, Satan*! You are an offense to Me, for you are not mindful of the things of God, but the things of men.'" Here Jesus is describing his future death and resurrection to his disciples. Peter then remonstrates that such a thing could never happen, far be it from Jesus that this would happen to him! Of course, Peter was not fully aware that this was part of God's divine plan of redemption, and thus, unconsciously inspired by Satan rebuffs Jesus. Jesus responds not to Peter but to Satan, commanding him to get behind him, to cease and desist from tempting Peter. Satan can only obey, just as he was only permitted to strike Job with illness and scars but was barred from going so far to take his life.

Satan is so under God's control that Rev 20:7 describes the devil as sitting in jail until the end of the thousand-year reign of Christ when he will be released. Released to do God's will that has been permitted him to do. God has put Satan into time-out like a colicky brat until his time has come.

We must understand that God's mercy is infinite in the sense that it flows from an infinite being. However, we must not make the mistake that individuals or whole people can keep on sinning forever, without any consequences. If people keep sinning so greatly for so long, God may eventually remove his restraining mercies from certain people, and hand them over to their sins. Revelation 22:11 says, "He who is unjust, let him be unjust still; he who is filthy, let him be filthy still; he who is righteous, let him be righteous still; he who is holy, let him be holy still." God truly loves everyone and brings up his sun on both the evil and the good (Matt 5:45). God gives every person a certain amount of grace and doesn't allow people to become hellish demons while here on earth. But if people cross a certain line and abuse God's grace, then he hands them over to their lusts, their passions, and their sins.[4]

This only means that God allows certain people to become manifestly reprobate in abandoning them to their sins. It is a kind of prejudgment upon these people. It doesn't mean, as in Flowers view, that anybody had the capability to choose God, and since they rejected him, they were given over to their sin. Every person is born in sin, and every reprobate is on their course to hell. Yet the elect are those whom God graciously lifts out of their course to hell and redeems them.

In fact, if God were not in total control of evil events happening, it would mean that he is not truly God. It would mean that according to the Manichaean scenario Satan could possibly slip out from under God's control or even have a chance of triumphing over God. Banish the thought! God controls all events to such a minute extent, that despite the evil men scheming to do evil deeds, God does not permit them to carry them out, but rather turns them into good for his own glory. Evil cannot catch God off guard.

Let's think about the converse: why do the wicked seem to prosper? There is a clue from Rom 2:5–6: "But in accordance with your hardness and your impenitent heart you are treasuring up for yourself wrath in the day of wrath and revelation of the righteous judgment of God, who 'will render to each one according to his deeds.'" What this means is that even though

---

4. Sproul, *Righteous Shall Live by Faith*, 32–33.

A Critique of Provisionism

the wicked are blessed by God (since God loves all men and brings up the sun on both the good and the bad), these blessings will ultimately turn into curses on judgment day. Why? Because every time God gave blessings even to the wicked, they were ungrateful and rejected God. The more the wicked prosper, the more blessings they receive. But the more ungrateful they are will be reason to damn them further and further into the deepest pits of hell.[5]

Romans 8:28 says, "And we know that *all things work together for good to those who love God, to those who are the called according to His purpose.*"

Let us now examine several passages of Scripture where it appears that God apparently causes bad events to happen for a greater purpose.

Moses and Pharaoh

The first such passage of Scripture deals with Moses and Pharaoh. We have dealt with this part of the Bible before, so we won't get into too much detail. Here God hardens Pharaoh's heart to show his glory in freeing his own people from the most powerful despot of the world at that time and to serve as an example of his power and might for subsequent generations.

Joseph Sold into Slavery

The next passage of Scripture deals with Joseph being sold into slavery by his brothers in Gen 37. Joseph had to go through many hardships, even being cast into prison after he was falsely accused of sexually assaulting Potiphar's wife (Gen 39:20). But God was with Joseph, even when he was cast into the well, and when he was in prison. The Lord guided events so that Joseph prospered (Gen 39:23). It was part of God's plan for Joseph to be sold into slavery, since in the end he was able to store up much food for the Jewish people in the land of Goshen when there was famine in the land of Israel. This was not just God's foreknowledge of future events that would transpire concerning Joseph and his people, but rather it all happened by God's design.[6]

Let us read what Joseph says about these events in Gen 45:5–8: "But now, do not therefore be grieved or angry with yourselves because you sold

---

5. Sproul, *Righteous Shall Live by Faith*, 256.
6. Piper, *Providence*.

me here; for *God sent me before you* to preserve life. For these two years the famine has been in the land, and there are still five years in which there will be neither plowing nor harvesting. And *God sent me before you* to preserve a posterity for you in the earth, and to save your lives by a great deliverance. *So now it was not you who sent me here, but God*; and He has made me a father to Pharaoh, and lord of all his house, and a ruler throughout all the land of Egypt."

How intriguing! Joseph says that even though his own brothers had deliberately sold him into slavery, it was God himself who sent him to the land of Egypt. He says this three times, so this is very emphatic. It is simply not true that humans behave as independent, sovereign actors as Flowers's provisionism imagines. What evil Joseph's brothers had planned against him God had truly turned it around into a real blessing! How great is our sovereign God that he can bring good out from evil.

David Numbers Israel

In 2 Sam 24:1–2 King David numbers his people by way of a national census. Israel had again displeased the Lord, who then moved David to number them (figure 3). Why was a census such a displeasing thing to do? King David was at the height of his power. He had conquered all of his enemies, and he had riches in abundance. God had truly blessed him. However, David's heart may have swelled with pride, attributing God's graces to his own personal glory. He may have looked upon the people of Israel as his own people, not something that God had given to him. And so, he wanted to count all his people to bask in his own glory.[7]

Apparently, it was a great hassle for people to go through. There was a lot of red tape, rules, and regulations. It wasn't so easy as today when everything can be done electronically. Soldiers had to march out to each and every single house in the country and ask how many people lived in each house. Sometimes people weren't at home, sometimes they would have been counted twice. It would have been somewhat of a fool's errand. Imagine asking a farmer to count the exact number of blades of grass in his largest wheat field.

---

7. Pink, *Life of David*, 356–57.

A Critique of Provisionism

Figure 3

God later punished David for his misdeed. God allowed David to choose from among three forms of suffering: seven years famine, three months of fleeing from his enemies, or a plague lasting three days. But wait! Did we not read in verse 1 that it was God himself who moved David to number his people? Indeed, it is. It is as if we could hear Flowers condemning such an idea that God would punish someone for doing something that he himself made them do. Flowers would be indignant because of the seeming injustice of it all. Yet, this is exactly what the Bible says. But interestingly, in 2 Sam 24:10 we read that David accuses himself of committing this great misdeed against his own people. We read "*I have sinned greatly in what I have done*; but now, I pray, O Lord, *take away the iniquity of Your servant, for I have done very foolishly*." Here David himself owns up to the sin of counting his people *as if it has been his own deed!* Here we have an example of concurrence, God acting together with man at the same time.

The Potter's Promise

A Lying Spirit in the Prophets' Mouths

Next is the story of the demise of King Ahab of Israel found in 1 Kgs 22:1–40. Ahab was an evil king who did what was displeasing to God. He had been eyeing the region of Ramoth Gilead for several years, believing that it was rightfully his. However, he was no match alone for the king of Syria who occupied that territory. Therefore, he had Jehoshaphat, king of Judah, come up to assist him in his endeavor. Two against one will do the job, thought Ahab.

Once Jehoshaphat was in the court of Israel, the four hundred false prophets got to work to work trying to convince King Ahab that his plans will be fruitful should he go up to attack Ramoth Gilead. Imagine a courtroom full of yes-men, each trying to outdo one another in persuading both kings to attack the enemy. It must have been a menagerie with prophets pulling off stunts, using iron horns to show how King Ahab would gore the Syrians to death.

It is at this point when the prophet Micaiah is summoned to ask him what the Lord had to say (figure 4). Micaiah alone was a true prophet of God. He always told the truth. But for that he was hated by King Ahab, because he only prophesied evil and never good (verse 8). This must have been because Ahab was evil and often incurred God's displeasure and even wrath. It got to the point that Ahab was so recalcitrant in his heart and so darkened in his understanding that he never inquired the word of God anymore. Ahab was an apostate king who had turned his back on God for good and was unable even to repent. The only reason Ahab inquired of God was a token formalism.

That is why we get a glimpse of the heavenly throne room in verses 19–23. Here we get to see behind the veil into the secret decretive will of God. The Lord asks his host, "Who will persuade Ahab to go up, that he may fall at Ramoth Gilead?" Woe be unto the man against whom the Lord takes concrete steps to cause his demise! Here we see that God actually commands one of his own heavenly host to go and delude King Ahab to finally bring an end to his ungodly reign. And so, one of the spirits went and did as God directed him to do. And in verse 23 we read that God had declared disaster upon King Ahab.

God is a loving God, but ultimately even his great patience can end. Second Thessalonians 2:11 says that "and for this reason God will send them strong delusion, that they should believe the lie." Isaiah 66:4 says, "So

A Critique of Provisionism

will I choose their delusions, and bring their fears on them; because, when I called, no one answered, when I spoke they did not hear; *but they did evil before My eyes, and chose that in which I do not delight.*" In Lam 2:14 we read, "Your prophets have seen for you false and deceptive visions; *they have not uncovered your iniquity*, to bring back your captives, *but have envisioned for you false prophecies and delusions.*" Israel many times sinned greatly against God, to the point of being incorrigible. Humans can get to the point that their hearts are so hardened against God, that he simply turns men over to their own darkness. In Romans 1:21–22 we read "because, although they knew God, they did not glorify Him as God, nor were thankful, but became futile in their thoughts, and their foolish hearts were darkened. Professing to be wise, they became fools." This is real. Men by their own choice reject God and thus suffer the consequences of their own folly.

Figure 4

Job's Sufferings

The book of Job is a good way to understand God's sovereignty in the face of evil. In it, we get a glimpse of God behind the scenes of the everyday life of Job, a God-fearing man who serves the Lord and offers sacrifices for

The Potter's Promise

them regularly. In this book we read about a challenge between God and Satan, who tries to defy God by saying that Job only loves God because he blesses Job. Should God withdraw his blessings over Job's life, then Job will turn away from God (Job 1:9–11).

God permits Satan to take away all of Job's possessions, his livestock, his goods, and even his family. Furthermore, Job underwent horrendous physical sufferings (figure 5). For Satan to take away Job's life would have been just one more calamity, and Satan would have well been more than willing to kill Job. But, as we can see, Satan cannot do more than what is allowed him by Almighty God.

Satan is the god of this age (2 Cor 4:4). He has *temporarily* been given the realms of this world, as we can read in Matt 4:8–9 when he takes Jesus up to the top of the mountains and shows all of the kingdoms of the world and their glory in a moment, saying that he can give them to anyone whom he wishes (Luke 4:6). *This is a lie*, since Satan himself was only given these kingdoms for a limited amount of time. He is a creature and thus has only received what he has been given by God.

In a similar vein, the rider of the red horse in Rev 6:4 was also *only granted* to take peace from the earth and to kill people with the sword. In Rev 6:8, Death and Hades are only given power to kill a fourth of all the earth. Lastly, the beast in Rev 13:7 was also only granted authority to war against the saints, and to have authority over every tribe, tongue, and nation.

Figure 5

A Critique of Provisionism

And indeed, in Job 2:9–10 Job humbly tells his wife that they should receive *both the good and the bad* from the hand of the Lord: "Then his wife said to him, 'Do you still hold fast to your integrity? Curse God and die!' But he said to her, 'You speak as one of the foolish women speaks. Shall we indeed accept good from God, and shall we not accept adversity?' In all this Job did not sin with his lips." Can you see here that the Bible clearly describes how even bad things are from God—for a purpose? Bad things are not just random events striking out at us from the dark. Though we may not understand why bad things come our way, we should keep our trust in the Lord that he has an ulterior purpose with them, even for our good.

Though Job is suffering terrible sorrows and pains, yet he does not lose faith in God. God is sovereign and can turn his misery to good. God first elevated Job to great honor and wealth, but then took it all away to prove that Job would not leave him in his wager with Satan.[8] It is also important to see here that Job can accept both the good and the bad from God's hand. God gives them both because all things come from him (and nothing from Satan). Arminians, on the other hand, would ascribe the evil coming from Satan. As such, they could even question why God did not have the power to stop all evil from happening. If they were consistent, they would have to concede that God is powerless to help them. But in the end, Job is blessed even more than in the beginning. He gets all his sheep, camels, oxen, and donkeys back. He is given three sons and seven daughters. He even lives on for 140 years and even sees his children and grandchildren for four generations (Job 42:12–17).

A similar thing happened when Jesus was betrayed, abandoned, and denied by the disciples to the Jewish leaders by Judas and Peter. In the latter case, in Luke 22:31–32 Jesus tells Peter that Satan had asked to sift Peter to see what was truly in him. Jesus knew that Peter would deny him three times, caving to Satan's temptation. But that is why Jesus prayed for Peter so that his faith would not fail and even afterwards that he would strengthen his brothers in the faith. Both Peter and Job were sifted by Satan, something which God in his providence allowed to happen, but during which God did not allow Satan to overstep his boundaries. Satan was ultimately kept at bay, Job was blessed, and Peter recovered in his faith, so much so that he became a strong Christian leader afterwards.

---

8. Morris, *Remarkable Record*.

Roboam Makes His People Suffer

First Kings 11:1—12:24 describe a turn of events where the Lord punishes Israel for King Solomon's disobedience to God, for taking a multitude of foreign wives to himself. God strictly forbade this to the Jewish people, warning them that they would surely turn their hearts after foreign gods (verse 2). Solomon had seven hundred wives and three hundred concubines and built altars to the gods Chemosh of Moab and Molech of Ammon (verse 7). Thus, king Solomon instituted pagan idol worship in Israel and thus turned many away from the worship of the true God. For this grievous sin God foretold Solomon that he would take away his kingdom and give it to his servant, Jeroboam (verses 12–13). Furthermore, the descendants of the house of David will be afflicted, but not forever, for David's sake (1:39).

God then raised up adversaries against King Solomon to harass him: Hadad the Edomite, Rezon the son of Eliadah, and Jeroboam the son of Nebat, a mighty man of valor, who became a high-ranking officer of the labor force of Joseph. In 1 Kgs 11:35, God prophecies to Jeroboam via Ahijah the prophet that he would receive ten of the twelve tribes of Israel.

After Solomon, Roboam became king in Israel. When consulting with the elders of the land, they suggested to the king that he be the nation's servant and speak good words to the people so that the people would be his servants always (12:7). However, Roboam rejected the counsel of the elders and listened rather to the young men that he had grown up with and promised to increase the load on the people and chastise them with scourges (12:4). In verse 12:15 we then read, "So the king did not listen to the people; for *the turn of events was from the Lord*, that He might fulfill His word, which the Lord had spoken by Ahijah the Shilonite to Jeroboam the son of Nebat." Roboam then increases the taxes on the people who then revolt, and force Roboam to flee to Jerusalem. Jeroboam then returns from exile in Egypt to where he had fled before Solomon and then becomes king of Israel. This then sets the stage for the divided kingdom, leading up to the exile in Babylon later in 587 BC.

What we see here again is God raising up an evil man, Roboam, to afflict his people, but as punishment for their idolatry. God foreordains evil to come to pass, but this is a part of his judgment against his own people.

A Critique of Provisionism

The Fall of Jerusalem

Jerusalem fell in the year 586 BC. The events leading up to the fall of the great city are described in 2 Kgs 24:18—25:30. King Jehoiachin of Judah had done evil in the sight of the Lord, just like his predecessor, King Jehoiakim had done (24:19-20). The time had finally come for God to punish Israel. Thus, he raised up Nebuchadnezzar, the king of Babylon, who came and besieged the city and destroyed it completely. He conquered the city, took the king captive, and plundered all the fine articles in the temple of God which Solomon had built. He took all the mighty men, the leaders, the craftsmen, and the smiths as captives to Babylon, leaving only the poorest people behind.

Interestingly, in verse 2 of 2 Kgs 24, we read that it was the Lord who had done this thing: "*And the Lord sent against him raiding bands of Chaldeans, bands of Syrians, bands of Moabites, and bands of the people of Ammon; He sent them against Judah to destroy it, according to the word of the Lord which He had spoken by His servants the prophets.*" Verse 20 of chapter 24 that God had done all this because of the anger of the Lord, that God had finally cast them out of his presence, and to send his people to Babylon.

In the book of Daniel, chapter 1, we read about Daniel and his three companions: Hananiah, Mishael, and Azariah. These four noble youths were deported from Israel to Babylon to be reeducated according to the literature of the Chaldeans (the Babylonians). They were even given Chaldean names to honor the Babylonian gods. For example, Azariah was given the name Abed-Nego, which means "servant of [the god] Nego." It must have been humiliating for Daniel and his three friends to undergo such a thing. It would have been a disgrace. But still, he endured the humiliation, because in the previous chapters we see that Jerusalem's fall was from God.

In verses 8-20, Daniel and his three companions decided that they would not take part of the king's table, and that he would not eat his food, but rather eat vegetables and drink water. In other words, this was a fast that Daniel undertook for God. Eating at table with others means that you have fellowship with one another at table. Though Daniel was being forcefully reeducated, he did not want to capitulate entirely. Yet after a trial period of ten days (verse 14), Daniel and his companions were found to be better in appearance than all the other young men at the king's court. After their training they were also found to have better wisdom and understanding than all the others. This was a sign that God was able to *physically* sustain

Daniel during his fast. Verse 17 also says that God also gave them the superior understanding. Truly God was with Daniel and was sustaining him and the Jewish people during their deportment in Babylon until they could go home to worship him.

The Father Sacrifices the Son

Bad things happen to all people. We lose a job, suffer an accident, or even our children may die. Hebrews 4:15 says this: "For we do not have a High Priest who cannot sympathize with our weaknesses, but was in all points tempted as we are, yet without sin." Just as we suffered so did Christ. Just as people may thwart us, so the Jewish leaders thwarted Christ. Just as we weep and have sorrow, so did Christ. But most importantly of all, Christ went to the cross and died a horrible death for us and bore our sins so that we would not have to die. This is the focal event of all human history. It was the greatest sin ever to kill the Son of God, yet it brought God the greatest glory.

And it was all part of God's foreordained plan! Acts 2:23 says, "Him, being delivered by the *determined purpose and foreknowledge of God*, you have taken by lawless hands, have crucified, and put to death." Revelation 13:8 says, "All who dwell on the earth will worship him, whose names have not been written in the Book of Life of the Lamb *slain from the foundation of the world*." This indicates that it was God's plan from before the beginning of the world to sacrifice his Son, Jesus Christ to save men from their sin. Isaiah 53:10 says, "Yet *it pleased the Lord to bruise Him*; He has put Him to grief. When You make His soul an offering for sin." Luke 22:22 says, "And truly the Son of Man goes as it has been determined, but woe to that man by whom He is betrayed!" It was determined beforehand for Jesus to die on the cross, yet his betrayer, Judas, shall be held accountable for it. Jesus' death is part of God's plan, but God is not held responsible for this sin (figure 6).

This means that Jesus' death wasn't a random act. It wasn't "plan B" in God's great scheme of things. Jesus didn't just come up with the idea. Rather God willfully, purposefully sacrificed his own Son as part of his plan to save men. Just like Job, we might have to take the evil from God's hands together with the good. But here we see that God the Father purposefully sacrificed his Son so that we could reconcile with him and have peace. Since Jesus himself partakes of the worst kind of suffering, Arminians cannot argue that God randomly metes out unfair punishment to people—his Son took part in it as well! Just as Christ's suffering led to the salvation of many, our

A Critique of Provisionism

suffering also has an ultimate purpose, even if we may not yet understand it. God took the worst sin ever committed and turned it into the greatest act ever, accomplishing the salvation of millions.

Figure 6

Paul's Thorn in the Flesh

In 2 Cor 12:7–10 Paul writes:

> And lest I should be exalted above measure by the abundance of the revelations, a thorn in the flesh was given to me, a messenger of Satan to buffet me, lest I be exalted above measure. Concerning this thing I pleaded with the Lord three times that it might depart from me. And He said to me, "My grace is sufficient for you, for My strength is made perfect in weakness." Therefore most gladly I will rather boast in my infirmities, that the power of Christ may rest upon me. Therefore I take pleasure in infirmities, in reproaches, in needs, in persecutions, in distresses, for Christ's sake. For when I am weak, then I am strong.

Paul was given a thorn in the flesh, to undergo sickness, reproach, want, persecution, and distress. Paul wanted God to remove the thorn from his flesh three times. It would make perfect sense for God to remove this evil from God if he was truly good, right? According to Arminian logic. But God would not remove it from him. God wanted to teach Paul that his grace is sufficient for everything, and that he should always rely on God in all things, so that Paul would not become proud. God can even use suffering for our benefit.

As we have seen from these nine lengthy descriptions, God does indeed intend, cause, and bring about bad things. But he does not do so just to wantonly spread suffering and destruction. Rather, all these things happen for a greater, good purpose that we may not understand yet. God is good, he is sovereign, and he is fully in control. God knows and controls every single event in the universe. The devil has no control and no authority whatsoever. We are all fulfilling God's plans, not the devil's plans.

5

The Potter's Word

"What shall we say then? Is there unrighteousness with God? Certainly not! For He says to Moses, 'I will have mercy on whomever I will have mercy, and I will have compassion on whomever I will have compassion.' So then it is not of him who wills, nor of him who runs, but of God who shows mercy."

(Romans 9:14–16)

Introduction

Chapter five of Flowers's book is a long interpretation of three key biblical passages the support Calvinist doctrine: John 6, Eph 1, and Rom 8–9. So important is this for Flowers, that he devoted literally half of his book trying to bring out a non-Calvinist interpretation of these passages. Therefore, in the following, I shall examine his interpretation of these three chapters of the Bible and show why they do not support provisionism, but rather the Calvinist view.

The Potter's Word

John 6: How Does the Father Draw People to Himself?

The important passage of Scripture that we are dealing with here is John 6:37–46:

> "All that the Father gives Me will come to Me, and the one who comes to Me I will by no means cast out. For I have come down from heaven, not to do My own will, but the will of Him who sent Me. This is the will of the Father who sent Me, that of all He has given Me I should lose nothing, but should raise it up at the last day. And this is the will of Him who sent Me, that everyone who sees the Son and believes in Him may have everlasting life; and I will raise him up at the last day." The Jews then complained about Him, because He said, "I am the bread which came down from heaven." And they said, "Is not this Jesus, the son of Joseph, whose father and mother we know? How is it then that He says, 'I have come down from heaven'?" Jesus therefore answered and said to them, "Do not murmur among yourselves. No one can come to Me unless the Father who sent Me draws him; and I will raise him up at the last day. It is written in the prophets, 'And they shall all be taught by God.' Therefore everyone who has heard and learned from the Father comes to Me. Not that anyone has seen the Father, except He who is from God; He has seen the Father."

Flowers gives the following surprising interpretation to verse 38: "God's will was for Jesus to come 'down from heaven' and train a preselected group of Israelites (those given to Him to be apostles) to carry the gospel to the world and establish His church after He is raised from the dead."[1] Flowers bases this interpretation on verse 45, which says that they shall all be taught by God. Flowers states that this refers to the twelve disciples *alone*,[2] who witnessed Jesus walk on water, heal people, and feed the masses.[3]

It seems that Flowers claims that the only reason Jesus came down from heaven was to put on a private miracle show, meant exclusively for the disciples' eyes alone. This is clearly false, as the four Gospels clearly describe how multitudes heard Jesus' preaching (see the Beatitudes in Matt 5), and the feeding of thousands of people that Flowers himself references.

---

1. Flowers, *Potter's Promise*, 75.
2. Note here that Flowers interprets the word "all" in John 6:45 in a distributive manner (meaning that certain groups of people are taught by God), the way many Calvinists interpret this word in many cases.
3. Flowers, *Potter's Promise*, 74.

A Critique of Provisionism

Furthermore, the phrase "It is written in the prophets" in verse 45 references Isa 54:13: "*All your children* shall be taught by the Lord, and great shall be the peace of your children." All of Israel's children shall be taught by the Lord, not just twelve select disciples. This contradicts Flowers's framework within which he interprets John 6:37–46.

Flowers's interpretation of these verses has nothing at all to do with the text and is only eisegesis. In the wider context of John 6 Jesus is talking to the Israelites who had just witnessed his multiplying the bread to feed them. In verse 35 Jesus transitions from feeding the people with literal bread to feeding them with spiritual bread, namely preaching the gospel to them: "He who comes to me shall never hunger, and he who believes in Me shall never thirst." This verse alone refutes Flowers's premise that Jesus did not come to evangelize but only to train the disciples. In verses 37 Jesus says that he shall by no means cast out those who the Father had given him. This is salvific language. What Jesus is talking about is that if someone repents and comes to him, he shall never be rejected. Jesus reaffirms this in verse 39, where he says that he will lose no one whom the Father has given him. Not only will Jesus not reject the repentant sinner, he will also never lose him afterwards, and will raise him up on the last day as we read in verse 44. This means that if the sinner repents, his salvation is guaranteed.

John speaks about the people given to the Son by the Father in verses 37 and 39 as a transaction that is being done both in the present, but also in the past. Those who trust in Christ in the present do so because they have been chosen by the Father and given to the Son in a second stage of redemption.[4] Acts 13:48 also corroborates this: "Now when the Gentiles heard this, they were glad and glorified the word of the Lord. And as many as had been *appointed* to eternal life believed."[5] Song 1:4 also describes how men come to Christ: "Draw me away! We will run after you!" First God will draw people to himself and cause them to believe in him. When men believe, they will then run towards God. They will come to him. This is yet another example of concurrence, when God's will and man's will act together, with God

---

4. Henry, *Commentary*, John 6:28–59.

5. Free will theologians may dispute the meaning of the word "appointed": τεταγμένοι (tetagmenoi) in Acts 13:48. However, this word also appears in Rom 13:1: "Let every soul be subject to the governing authorities. For there is no authority except from God, and the authorities that exist are appointed by God," where the word appointed is also τεταγμέναι (tetagmenai). This word clearly denotes a selection or designation of certain people on the part of God.

initiating the act of faith, but producing such a faith in men that they now choose to follow God of their newly regenerated free will.

In this passage of Scripture, we read about how God is truly the one who takes the initiative in salvation. It is he who draws sinners to him, as we read in verse 44. In fact, verse 44 indicates that the reason people come to Jesus is *not through their own freewill decision*. Calvin rightly comments that if it only when we are drawn to the Father that we begin to come to Christ, this leaves no room for any prior kind of preparation for faith.[6]

Wesley himself and subsequent Arminian Methodists understood the force of this verse that they were compelled to come up with the concept of prevenient grace. Methodists, such as Wesley, are two-point "Calvinists" in that they accept the doctrine of total depravity and perseverance of the saints. They realize that people truly are dead in their sins and cannot, by themselves come to Christ. They need God to revive them and bring them into a state of grace where they can now cooperate with God in salvation and choose Jesus. They paint a picture of God fishing out spiritually dead people, reviving them, and then putting them in a position whereby with their newly enlightened minds are capable of either choosing or rejecting Jesus.[7] Since Wesleyan Arminianism claims that God loves all, therefore God wishes to give all the possibility of salvation by choosing the Son. However, verse 44 states that unless the Father draws someone, he cannot be saved. The "unless" implies that God draws some, but does not draw others, but leaves them in their sin.

Moreover, in verses 37 and 39 we read about how prior to the sinner coming to Jesus, these self-same sinners were given to him by the Father.[8] This makes sense only in the light of Calvinist doctrine. First, God the Father before time began elected some to salvation, whom he then gives to the Son, who will preserve the elect until the last day when they shall be raised up. Here we have unconditional election, irresistible grace, and perseverance of the saints in these verses![9]

---

6. Calvin, *Commentary on John*, ch. 12, part 7.

7. Olson, *Arminian Theology*, 75–76.

8. Here "everyone that sees the Son and believes in Him" in the Greek is πᾶς ὁ θεωρῶν τὸν υἱὸν καὶ πιστεύων εἰς αὐτόν. More specifically, here the word πιστεύων (pisteuon) is a participle, which denotes certain people who are believing (in Jesus). This is the exact same phrase which is also found in John 3:16: πᾶς ὁ πιστεύων εἰς αὐτόν. It means that all those who are believing in Jesus shall not perish but shall have eternal life. This word does not denote an "if-then" condition, that *if* you believe in Jesus, *then* you shall be saved.

9. White, *Potter's Freedom*, 155–56.

A Critique of Provisionism

In order to harmonize John 6:37–46 with free will, some Arminians say that Jesus raises all people to himself, not just an elect group, as stated in John 12:32: "And I, if I am lifted up from the earth, will draw all peoples to Myself." All people are drawn, but only some choose. However, this misses the thrust of John 6:37–46 in that the whole point of some people, given to him by the Father is to raise them up on the last day, without losing a single one. If the Arminian logic holds, then this leads to universal salvation, which we know is false. Thus, John 12:32 can only mean that Jesus draws to himself all kinds of people, not each and every single person in the world. This is the same logic that is used in John 3:16 and also John 6:37, 39, and 45.

Ephesians 1: Chosen for What?

In Eph 1:3–14 we read:

> Blessed be the God and Father of our Lord Jesus Christ, who has blessed us with every spiritual blessing in the heavenly places in Christ, just as He chose us in Him before the foundation of the world, that we should be holy and without blame before Him in love, having predestined us to adoption as sons by Jesus Christ to Himself, according to the good pleasure of His will, to the praise of the glory of His grace, by which He made us accepted in the Beloved. In Him we have redemption through His blood, the forgiveness of sins, according to the riches of His grace which He made to abound toward us in all wisdom and prudence, having made known to us the mystery of His will, according to His good pleasure which He purposed in Himself, that in the dispensation of the fullness of the times He might gather together in one all things in Christ, both which are in heaven and which are on earth—in Him. In Him also we have obtained an inheritance, being predestined according to the purpose of Him who works all things according to the counsel of His will, that we who first trusted in Christ should be to the praise of His glory. In Him you also trusted, after you heard the word of truth, the gospel of your salvation; in whom also, having believed, you were sealed with the Holy Spirit of promise, who is the guarantee of our inheritance until the redemption of the purchased possession, to the praise of His glory.

The Potter's Word

At first glance, the Calvinist interpretation of this passage of Scripture seems clear cut: God the Father chose us before the foundation of the world (verse 4). He predestined us to adoption as his sons, to holiness, according to his purpose (verses 5 and 11). As such, God's purpose in election can only be of pure love; to bring his elect into a personal relationship with himself.[10]

Similar to John 6:37–46, here also Flowers tries to defuse the Calvinist interpretation of this verse by claiming that it is only about "God predetermining the spiritual blessings for those who are in Christ through believing the word of truth."[11] In other words, once someone is saved by their freewill choice, then their course is set to become holy, blameless, and to be adopted as sons.

However, when the language of these verses is examined more closely, we see that they do not emphasize human volition or choice, rather the good pleasure of God's will and his purposes. Not any goodness or virtue that was foreseen in the elect.[12] No thought, act, word, or deed can sway God to elect anyone. He predestines according to the pleasure of his will (verse 5). God purposed his will in himself (verse 9). God works all things to the counsel of his own will, not our will (verse 11).

When we look at the wider context of God's electing purpose, in Eph 2:1–10 we read:

> And you He made alive, who were dead in trespasses and sins, in which you once walked according to the course of this world, according to the prince of the power of the air, the spirit who now works in the sons of disobedience, among whom also we all once conducted ourselves in the lusts of our flesh, fulfilling the desires of the flesh and of the mind, and were by nature children of wrath, just as the others. But God, who is rich in mercy, because of His great love with which He loved us, even when we were dead in trespasses, made us alive together with Christ (by grace you have been saved), and raised us up together, and made us sit together in the heavenly places in Christ Jesus, that in the ages to come He might show the exceeding riches of His grace in His kindness toward us in Christ Jesus. For by grace you have been saved through faith, and that not of yourselves; it is the gift of God, not of works, lest anyone should boast. For we are His workmanship, created in

---

10. Erdman, *Epistle of Paul*, 31.
11. Flowers, *Potter's Promise*, 79.
12. Erdman, *Epistle of Paul*, 29.

A Critique of Provisionism

Christ Jesus for good works, which God prepared beforehand that we should walk in them.

If we focus especially on verses 8–10, we will understand several things. First, that salvation is not a work, but rather it is 100 percent a gift. Because it is not a work, it is not of ourselves. Salvation is not human in origin. The elect are all God's workmanship, created to do good works. These are special works in that they are not of our own making but rather ones that God had predestined for us beforehand that we should walk in them. These verses underscore how everything is by God's grace. Literally everything. Even the breath we take is given to us. Even our good deeds, and even our choices have been predetermined by God to fit his great overarching plan, to the praise of the glory of his grace.

Other Arminians try to avoid the clear meaning of verse 8 by saying that it is not faith that is the gift of God, but rather salvation in a broader sense. Let us look at this verse in Greek: "τῇ γὰρ χάριτί ἐστε σεσῳσμένοι διὰ πίστεως· καὶ τοῦτο οὐκ ἐξ ὑμῶν, θεοῦ τὸ δῶρον" (te gar chariti este sesomenoi dia pisteos kai touto ouk ex humon Theou to doron) Here the word faith is πίστεως (pisteos), which is a feminine noun. The Calvinist interpretation would have the word it, τοῦτο (touto), a neutral word, refers to the word for salvation, σεσῳσμένοι (sesosmenoi), which is a participle. The argument is that since the gender of the word is neutral, it cannot refer to the word faith, which is feminine in gender. The two genders match, thus, "it" must refer to salvation, being entirely of God.[13]

In this manner the Arminian interpretation opens a loophole to allow salvation to be all of God, but that faith must be a response on man's part. This interpretation does nothing. Faith is part of the process of salvation, all the way from predestination down the order of events in the salvation of a person to the end stage of glorification.[14] Faith is one step in the process of salvation, and as such is also from God. If salvation as a whole is entirely from God, and as such, faith itself is also a gift from God.

---

13. Walls and Dongell, *Why I Am Not*, 77.

14. These stages in salvation constitute what is known as the *ordo salutis*, the series of events in a person's salvation, which will be covered in the next section.

The Potter's Word

Romans 8: What Is the Basis of God's Foreknowledge?

Flowers starts off his assessment of Rom 8 with a description of God's goodness towards those who love him. This is how Flowers defines his theology of provisionism: that there is a great cloud of witnesses (Heb 12:1) who bear witness to God's goodness. We can know that God will be good to us because he has proven his good character in the past, as he treated his servants Abraham, Moses, and David. Calvinists can readily believe in this; however, there are great differences as to whether or how God permits or even causes evil to happen. Flowers denies that God causes evil for his purposes. Rather, he redeems evil for a good purpose.[15]

Superficially, this may seem like a good resolution to God's purposes and the existence of evil. However, it leads to great problems, as we shall see. What about Adam's fall into sin in the garden of Eden? Was that not part of God's eternal purpose? According to Flowers, apparently not. Does this mean that Satan caught God, however good he may be, off guard? Was God not expecting the fall? Was it a cosmic accident? After all, since Flowers asserts that maximum goodness is part of God's character, then God should have prevented sin to come into the world at all. However, here we are, in a sin-ravaged world. God is neither ignorant, nor incompetent, and he is also good. God may have a deeper plan with sin coming into the world that we may never be fully aware of. As we have seen in chapter 4, sin is part of God's plan, as attested to be several verses of Scripture. But, since they are part of God's plan, they are also fully under God's full control, so much so that not a single detail escapes his notice.

What is also distressing about Flowers's position is that apparently evil is not under God's control. Satan, as an independent actor, is wreaking havoc in the world, roaring like a lion to devour who he may. In the provisionist system can God stop him? Or will they be forever locked in mortal combat, the one struggling against the other, where the one gets the upper hand over the other? As seen in chapter 4, this description of God actually fits the dualist religion of Manicheism.

Next, Flowers attempts to tackle the question of God's election against God's foreknowledge in Rom 8:29: "For whom He foreknew, He also predestined to be conformed to the image of His Son, that He might be the firstborn among many brethren." Here the great debate has been around what the foreknowledge of God means. Flowers follows the standard Arminian

---

15. Flowers, *Potter's Promise*, 83.

A Critique of Provisionism

interpretation of this verse, claiming that God foreknew those whom he would predestine from long ago, based on their choice for Jesus Christ. God sees those who choose him through the corridors of time and thus chooses these people because they had chosen him. In Acts 26:4–5, the Jews knew Paul's manner of life ever since his youthful days in Jerusalem. Similarly, God also will work for the good of those who love him, just as he had worked for the good of those whom he had known in previous times.[16]

This interpretation of Rom 8:29 is somewhat convoluted and stretched. Jesus plainly contradicts Flowers's view by saying that we did not choose him, but rather he chose us (John 15:16). The Bible plainly and simply says in this verse that God foreknew certain people, namely the elect, whom he then predestined for salvation. God foreknew certain people, *not how they would respond to him.*[17] In other words, God knows people, not *things about people*. Flowers and other Arminians are trying to make the text say something that it is not saying, based on what their theology dictates to them.[18] Flowers is adding to the Bible. "These he then called, whom he then justified, and also whom he also glorified" (Rom 8:30). Additionally, Flowers also concedes that foreknowledge can be interpreted as fore-loved, according to the Calvinist interpretation.[19]

Interestingly, even the act of glorification, a future event, is in the *past tense*. This means that God had planned the whole entire process of saving individuals had been planned in heaven from start to finish. Flowers responds to this argument that the context of Rom 8 does not clearly support the Calvinist interpretation. He also points out that the word glorified is in the aorist indicative, ἐδόξασεν (edochasen).[20] According to Flowers's provisionism, this should only mean that God glorified those who had trusted him in the past, thus God shall also glorify those who trust in him in the future. The fact that the word glorified is in the aorist, indicating an event in the past, does not derail the Calvinist interpretation. The use of the past tense to describe a future event can also be seen in Rev 13:8: "All who dwell on the earth will worship him, whose names have not been written in the Book of Life of the Lamb *slain from the foundation of the world.*" The Lamb

---

16. Flowers, *The Potter's Promise*, 86.
17. Peterson and Williams, *Why I am not an Arminian*, 76.
18. Steele, Thomas, Quinn, *The Five Points*, 158–59.
19. Flowers, *The Potter's Promise*, 86.
20. Flowers, *The Potter's Promise*, 93.

was slain before time began, as part of the eternal decree of God to save mankind. Yet Jesus, the Lamb of God was also slain during human history.

But what does the word foreknow mean? The Greek word is προγινώσκω (proginosko), which means to know beforehand, to foresee.[21] According to Thayer's Greek Lexicon, it means to elect or to predestinate. While this verb does designate prior objective knowledge, it also means a personal, intimate form of knowledge, just as God knows us now, but also knew us long ago before the foundation of the world, because he knew every single detail of our lives. This could only be because God knows all future events in detail. Surely, whatever God knows, those events shall come to pass, by virtue of God's knowing them. God's knowing his elect is enough for them to come to faith.

Two very different views of God collide in the Calvinist and the Arminian interpretation of God's foreknowledge. Does God merely play a passive role, only responding to our initiative of showing faith or is God in control, orchestrating all events in history for our salvation to ensure that we come to faith and never fall away finally? Which description of God portrays God as more powerful to help us in our need and distress? Which depiction is more loving? I think the answer is obvious. God planned out our salvation from before the beginning of time, and organized the movement of every atom so that we should come to faith. Calvinism portrays God's character more accurately than does the theology of provisionism.

Regeneration before Faith: A Key Element in the "Ordo Salutis"

While we are on this topic, it would be worthwhile interpreting the golden chain of Rom 8:30, the events of which are known as the *ordo salutis*. The *ordo salutis* is defined as the order of events that take place in a believer's life before and after he comes to faith. The Calvinist and freewill theology systems differ somewhat in the order of these events. The Calvinist system is depicted in figure 7.

---

21. "Strong's #4267."

A Critique of Provisionism

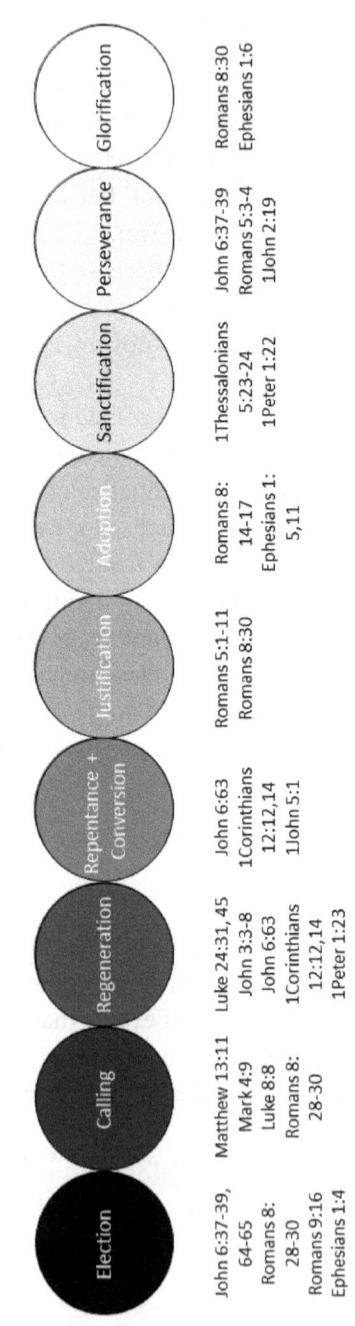

Figure 7

The Potter's Word

The main difference between the Arminian and the Calvinist system is whether faith (repentance and conversion) comes before or after regeneration. Different variants of the Arminian system may also differ in the placement of election. Whereas some Arminians believe that election happens before salvation, others may place election after faith and regeneration as a promise of God to elect man if man first chooses God.[22] In the Calvinist system since man cannot come to faith apart from God bestowing it upon him, regeneration (the new birth) must precede faith. God is always the first actor when man comes to faith. This is because ultimately faith is a gift given to us by God. The Arminian could argue that the reason he came to faith is because he sought God. The Calvinist could respond by asking, how is it that you came to seek God?[23] To this there is no good answer on the part of the Arminian, since there is none who seeks after God (Rom 3:11).

First Corinthians 4:7 asks the rhetorical question, "And what do you have that you did not receive?" Since we receive everything from God, faith is also such a gift. First John 5:1 also says, "Whoever *believes* that Jesus is the Christ *is born of God*, and everyone who loves Him who begot also loves him who is begotten of Him." Here belief comes about as a result of being born again by God. Acts 13:48 also indicates that election precedes faith and that only those will come to faith who have been chosen: "Now when the Gentiles heard this, they were glad and glorified the word of the Lord. *And as many as had been appointed to eternal life believed.*"

Also essential to the *ordo salutis* is how God's call to man is related to regeneration and faith. How can it be that people who are spiritually in Adam can even respond to God's call? As Rom 8:8 states, "So then, those who are in the flesh cannot please God." Jesus answers Nicodemus the Pharisee in John 3:3 regarding salvation that "most assuredly, I say to you, *unless one is born again*, he cannot see the kingdom of God." Men do not decide when and where they are born, so neither can man also decide when and where he is born again by the Spirit of God.[24] Or, how can a man on an operating table give himself a new heart? Ezekiel 36:26 says, "I will give you a new heart and put a new spirit within you; I will take the heart of stone out of your flesh and give you a heart of flesh." John 1:12–13 is quite emphatic that man's choice does not cause him to be born again by God: "But as many as received Him, to them He gave the right to become children of

---

22. Smith, *Systematic Theology*, 325–26.
23. Steele et al., *Five Points*, 172.
24. Murray, *Redemption Accomplished and Applied*, 99.

A Critique of Provisionism

God, to those who believe in His name: *who were born, not of blood, nor of the will of the flesh, nor of the will of man, but of God.*"

We must not look at regeneration in complete isolation. Although regeneration and the new birth are entirely God's work, they are connected to the fruits that follow thereafter. The fruits of the Spirit are love, joy, peace, long-suffering, kindness, goodness, faithfulness, gentleness, and self-control (Gal 5:22–23). Among these acts are *faithfulness*, or the turning to and trusting in God alone.

Does this mean that we are sent on a fool's errand? Demanding people to have faith who are incapable of it? Absolutely not. Calvinism upholds man's responsibility, and that man must have faith. Regeneration and faith go together and are inseparable from one another; they occur concomitantly. Let us preach the gospel as Jesus preached it: He who has ears to hear, let him hear! (Matt 11:5; 13:9)

Does Romans 9 Say What It Really Says?

With his provisionist theory in hand, Flowers attempts to tackle one of the classical loci of the Bible that clearly support the Calvinist worldview. He clearly must give some plausible interpretation of this chapter to avoid taking it at face value. However, he does this using several faulty assumptions and arguments, as have already become clear in his book. Flowers makes the claim that the Calvinistic interpretation of Rom 9 only showed up in the fifth century in Augustine's writings, and is thus a theological latecomer, a distortion of the gospel that the early Christians first believed.[25]

This has been dealt with in an earlier chapter, but it is still worth noting that in the early church some did not hold to a proper view of justification by grace. For example, according to Berkhof, many of the early church fathers attached great importance to faith manifesting itself in penitential deeds (e.g., almsgiving and abstinence). These deeds even had "expiatory value in atoning for sins committed after baptism," and that this contributed the entrance of legalistic Judaism into the church.[26]

First, Flowers one-sidedly overemphasizes human responsibility and human will, despite the clear biblical teaching of concurrence, as described in a previous section of this book. His second mistaken argument comes from this, namely that man hardens his own heart, and thereby calloused

---

25. Flowers, *Potter's Promise*, 103–4.
26. Berkhof, *History of Christian Doctrines*, 204–5.

himself against the will of God. God then takes these calloused individuals and judicially hardens them.[27] No. Man is born in sin, cut off from God, and is spiritually dead. It is God working in the heart of man that lifts him out of this calloused condition that he began in. In other words, all men are born bound to hell, and it takes a supernatural act of God to change their course towards eternal damnation.

Flowers makes it appear that man can only decline spiritually from a previous higher point: "Those judicially hardened and cut off are not born in this condition."[28] This optimistic view is simply not held by Scripture and employed by Flowers to invest man with free will. The truth is that Scripture teaches both election by God but also man's responsibility and freedom to choose him, in mystery. We must remember that God is both immanent (close-by), but also transcendent (distant), just as Jesus is both man and God. If either immanence or transcendence is overemphasized, this leads to theological imbalance and thus false teaching and heresy.

Flowers's third faulty argument is that he claims that people are indeed chosen, but only to serve God or carry out his will. This notion is hard to understand. How can Flowers conceive of sinners willfully obeying God? God chooses sinners, saves them, and then gives them a task to carry out. This can happen only with believers, never with unbelievers. Sinners reject God and rebel against his authority.

Lastly, Flowers argues that God chooses nations and peoples to bring about his redemptive plan.[29] This also makes no sense, since though God may choose nations, he still chooses *individuals within those nations*, such as Abraham. The Bible mentions individuals as elect, such as the elect lady in 2 John 1:1.

Romans 9 begins with Paul's anguish over his people's rejection of the gospel. Amazingly, he himself would wish to be cut off from God to save his own people from damnation. Flowers challenges the Calvinist viewpoint thus: "Despite Paul's explicit desire to perish in the place of these hardened Jews, five-point Calvinists teach that Christ does not share Paul's expressed intentions."[30]

Is this really true? Does God outdo the level of Paul's love towards his own countrymen? Are Calvinists unloving in restricting God's love from all

27. Flowers, *Potter's Promise*, 130.
28. Flowers, *Potter's Promise*, 130.
29. Flowers, *Potter's Promise*, 105, 114, 121, 128.
30. Flowers, *Potter's Promise*, 99.

people? Let's take Flowers's argument to its logical conclusion! If God's love is greater than Paul's, and if Christ died to save sinners, then should it not follow that Jesus saves all, and that all will be in heaven? Humanly thinking, why damn any single person to hell? To eternal damnation and suffering. God would be really, truly, infinitely loving if all would be saved down even to Judas, Hitler, and Stalin. But this is not so. God does not effectually save all, and so Flowers's argument falters. When Paul wishes himself to be cut off from God to save his fellow countrymen, he is humanly speaking. Our thoughts are not God's thoughts, and our ways are not his ways.

Now we come to the main point: national Israel has rejected her God. Indeed, Jer 3:6–10 says that God had divorced Israel. From then on, God turns to the gentile nations whom he will deal with. So then the question naturally arises: has God's word become ineffective in saving his own people? Does God not have the power to save? To those Jews who had received adoption, the glory, the covenants, the law, the service of God and the promises? God's very glory is on the line here.

With a sigh of relief, Paul declares, no! Because not all Israel are of Israel (Rom 9:6). No one can be called a child of God just because they are the seed of Abraham. God chose Israel to show how God deals with his people, and to produce the Messiah who would save his people from sin. God's choosing Israel goes beyond choosing a nation to the election and salvation of individuals within that nation. An individual Jew was never saved just because of his ethnic identity.

In other words, those who are saved, the true, spiritual Israel are not equated in an exact manner with national Israel. A smaller, distinct group of believing Jews within larger ethnic Israel will be saved. This is what Paul refers to when he writes in Rom 11:5: "Even so then, at this present time there is a remnant according to the election of grace." But true Israel includes not only believing Jews but *Christians as well* "as many as walk according to this rule, peace and mercy be upon them, and upon *the Israel of God*" (Gal 6:16).

With this knowledge in hand, we can thus make sense of Rom 11:25–26, which says, "For I do not desire, brethren, that you should be ignorant of this mystery, lest you should be wise in your own opinion, that *blindness in part has happened to Israel until the fullness of the Gentiles has come in. And so all Israel will be saved.*" The unbelieving Jews were blinded to the gospel, and rejected Jesus, their Messiah. Salvation then turned to the gentiles. When the last elect gentile comes to faith, then the number of the elect shall become full. In this way, both believing Jews and believing gentiles will come together in repentance to God, and so all true, spiritual Israel will be saved.[31] If libertarian free will was true, there would be no time limit as to who can still yet come to faith, whether it be a believing Jew or gentile. But this not what we read. All of these events happen according to God's setting up times for all events that come to pass.

Things get more intricate starting with Rom 9:9–13:

> For this is the word of promise: "At this time I will come and Sarah shall have a son." And not only this, but when Rebecca also had conceived by one man, even by our father Isaac (*for the children not yet being born, nor having done any good or evil, that the purpose of God according to election might stand, not of works but of Him who calls*), it was said to her, "The older shall serve the younger." As it is written, "*Jacob I have loved, but Esau I have hated.*"

Flowers declares that these verses do not teach that God hated an unborn baby for no apparent reason.[32] Apparently, Flowers is playing on the reader's emotions to reject the Calvinist position. Rather, as Flowers argues, individual salvation, one's eternal destiny, is not in view in these verses, but rather, national blessing, as in inheritance and land.[33]

In this way, Flowers places God's election into nations and not people. As we have seen earlier, this is faulty logic because God chooses individuals, not groups. This is because our individual actions are independent of one another. Furthermore, Flowers's interpretation of these verses is a huge detour from the surrounding context of Rom 9, and even the entire book of Romans, a book that deals with how one is saved, not about the fate of nations.[34] The whole entire book begins by Paul describing how he himself would rather be cut off for the sake of his countrymen.[35]

However, if we take a closer look at verse 11, we shall see how Flowers's interpretation falls flat. Before either Esau or Jacob was born, their eternal destiny had already been set; their salvation had been decided. This is because their salvation is independent of their *works*; their salvation does

---

31. Riddlebarger, *Case for Amillenialism*, 211–19.
32. Let us remember well that according to Flowers's theology, man must be able to choose God. Those who are inherently incapable of doing so, such as babies dying in the womb, are lost.
33. Flowers, *Potter's Promise*, 118.
34. Sproul, *Righteous Shall Live by Faith*, 284.
35. White, *Potter's Freedom*, 206.

A Critique of Provisionism

not depend upon whether they have done *good or evil*. Rather, salvation depends upon God's saving grace alone, *his sovereign election alone*.

Nevertheless, afterward, Flowers brings several examples of how the offspring of Edom, the Edomites, can experience God's love (Deut 23:7), because they are relatives of Israel. Also mentioned are the Ishmaelites, who became the father of the Arab nations, and did not receive the covenant, as did Isaac. Yet, Gen 17:20 promises that God will bless him, make him fruitful, multiply him exceedingly, and shall become a great nation. Lot also, was declared righteous (2 Pet 2:7), yet his future descendants, the Moabites and the Ammonites, were cursed for their opposition to Israel (Deut 23:3).

As we have seen earlier, not all Israel is of national Israel. Just because God chose Israel to be his people, national inheritance does not save. So also, a national curse does not necessarily mean that all those who belong to that people will be damned. For example, we know that Ruth was a Moabite (Ruth 1:4), who was even in the lineage leading from David to Jesus (Matt 1:5).

Rom 9:15–19 completely refutes the freewill Arminian position:

> For He says to Moses, "*I will have mercy on whomever I will have mercy, and I will have compassion on whomever I will have compassion.*" So then *it is not of him who wills*, nor of him who runs, but of God who shows mercy. For the Scripture says to the Pharaoh, "For this very purpose I have raised you up, that I may show My power in you, and that My name may be declared in all the earth." *Therefore He has mercy on whom He wills, and whom He wills He hardens.* You will say to me then, "Why does He still find fault? For who has resisted His will?"

As such, Flowers hardly gives any treatment to verses 18 and 19. He also goes so far as to say that "the apostle answers by reminding his readers that God's promise has never depended on the *desires and efforts* of unfaithful Israelites."[36] He claims that the "it" in verse 16 does not refer to salvation, but rather his *plan* for saving people. Flowers then falls back on his standard argument for judicial hardening of individuals.

But this argument completely ignores the context within which it rests. The previous verse states that God has mercy on those individual people on whom he has mercy. No reason whatsoever is given for why God chooses to save some people. It is wrapped up in his elective purposes, drawn up before eternity, unseen by human eyes, and unknown by the

---

36. Flowers, *Potter's Promise*, 128.

human understanding. This same concept is then repeated in verse 18, thus emphasizing the fact that individual salvation is in view here in verse 16. Lastly, verse 19 is a clear statement of the Calvinist doctrine of efficient (aka irresistible) grace: Paul asks the rhetorical question, who has resisted his will? The answer is, obviously, nobody, since no one can stand up to and resist God's almighty will. God will have his way with whomever he so wants. Let God's will be done, not ours.

Verse 17 illustrates individual salvation by describing how God hardened Pharaoh's heart. Flowers contends that Pharaoh's reprobation is not in purview here. However, the very fact that he kept the Israelites in slavery and revoked his word to let them go free ten times, and then had his army ominously drowned in the Red Sea, does not bode well for his salvation. Especially, since as some interpreters portray Pharaoh as Satan keeping God's people (the Israelites) in bondage, and then being set free by God himself through the Christ-figure Moses through the Red Sea, signifying the waters of baptism.

Flowers continues his attack against Calvinism with old arguments in interpreting Rom 9:20–23:

> But indeed, O man, who are you to reply against God? Will the thing formed say to him who formed it, "Why have you made me like this?" Does not the potter have power over the clay, from the same lump to make one vessel for honor and another for dishonor? What if God, wanting to show His wrath and to make His power known, endured with much longsuffering *the vessels of wrath prepared for destruction, and that He might make known the riches of His glory on the vessels of mercy, which He had prepared beforehand for glory.*

The teaching of these verses is very clear, so clear that the reader simply has to take them at face value. Paul is responding to a hypothetical opponent, who objects to God saving those whom he saves according to his own will, seemingly without man having any say in it. Man has absolutely no right whatsoever to criticize God for exercising his sovereign prerogatives in choosing whosoever he wills for whatever purpose he wills. This means that God has the right to elect some to salvation, and reprobate others to damnation; to prepare some vessels for glory, and others for destruction. Flowers claims that such a God is merely a grand puppet-master, turning some lumps of clay into believing men, and others into reprobates without affording them the possibility to change their moral state if they so wish, thus eliminating the responsibility of man.

A Critique of Provisionism

Calvinists indeed deny that man is a mere puppet in the hands of a divine puppet-master. We will have our cake and eat it too! To this the Calvinist can cite biblical references that simultaneously show God's election and man's responsibility, God's transcendence and immanence: Pss 37:23, 86:11, 119:113, Prov 16:1, 21:1, and Phil 2:12–13.

Interestingly, Flowers's counterargument is to say that God can shape pots of one kind into another kind. In other words, pots can change their state. This seems to imply that pots can go from reprobate to elect. For this, he cites Jer 18:1–6, of which the last three verses will be cited here: "And the vessel that he made of clay was marred in the hand of the potter; so he made it again into another vessel, as it seemed good to the potter to make. Then the word of the Lord came to me, saying: 'O house of Israel, can I not do with you as this potter?' says the Lord. *Look, as the clay is in the potter's hand, so are you in My hand, O house of Israel!*"[37]

Flowers implies here that a pot can be changed from one kind to another. But these verses say absolutely nothing about man changing his own eternal status before God. Only an ardent believer in freewill theology can read in his own beliefs into this passage. Paul's response to his freewill objector from Rom 9 even echoes here in the Old Testament as well. The Lord himself says, "Can I not do with you as this potter?" (Jer 18:6). Both in Rom 9:20–23 and in these verses, God is the sole actor. God can form pots for glory and for destruction. If he so wishes, he can make them into another vessel. All the way the clay is merely a passive lump in the hands of the divine Potter. God determines and directs our eternal destiny.

But Flowers keeps up the argument. He brings another verse from 2 Tim 2:20–21 to contrast the workings of the divine Potter even further: "But in a great house there are not only vessels of gold and silver, but also of wood and clay, some for honor and some for dishonor. *Therefore if anyone cleanses himself from the latter, he will be a vessel for honor, sanctified and useful for the Master, prepared for every good work.*"[38]

Here it seems that man himself can take an active role in determining his own fate. Has Flowers clinched the argument? Does this verse really mean that man can change himself from being a lost sinner to being saved? This interpretation would seem to contradict the plain teaching of Rom 9:20–23. Flowers ends up in a contradiction, because he is imposing his provisionist theology on these passages *which he takes in isolation from one*

---

37. Flowers, *Potter's Promise*, 135.

38. Flowers, *Potter's Promise*, 137; emphasis in original.

another. When taking Rom 9:20–23, Jer 18:1–6, and 2 Tim 2:20–21 in their full, overarching context, we shall see that they best conform to the Calvinist doctrine of concurrence.

In chapter 3 the three parables of Jesus in Luke 15 concerning the lost sheep, the lost coin, and the prodigal son were discussed. There we saw that Jesus does not tell these parables in random isolation from one another. Rather, he first describes the parable of the lost sheep and the lost coin first to describe man's inability. Then he describes the parable of the lost son who indeed decides to get out of the pigsty (which represents his sin) and turn back to his father, symbolizing repentance from sin and turning unto God. In the first two parables God is sovereign, electing and finding those who belong to him. But the third parable describe how man can truly decide out of his own free will to rise and go to God.

I say this as a Calvinist. All three parables are true at the same time. Both man's inability and his free will are true at the same time. God's election and man's choice go together in a mysterious way. This is concurrence. And so also God forms some lumps of clay for glory and others for dishonor (Rom 9:20–23; Jer 18:1–6), yet at the same time man can exercise free will and take part in his own sanctification (2 Tim 2:20–21).

Are there degrees in election? Flowers thinks so, in that God's chosen apostles from Israel were unique. He guards against taking what he describes as a self-centered approach to the interpretation of Rom 9:23–24, where God calls not only the Jews but also the gentiles.[39]

Why should there be degrees in election? Believers have all received the same Spirit (1 Cor 12:11) and all form one body (1 Cor 12:20). These apostles were called not because of anything special in themselves. Some, like Peter, were humble fishermen when the Lord came and called them. All believers share in the same ministry and call as that of the apostles. All are saved sinners, of which Paul calls himself the chief (1 Tim 1:15). Can the call of all believers be as great as that of the apostle? Jesus himself said, "Most assuredly, I say to you, he who believes in Me, the works that I do he will do also; and greater works than these he will do, because I go to My Father" (John 14:12).

Let us examine Rom 9:23 closer! "And that He might make known the riches of His glory on the vessels of mercy, *which He had prepared beforehand for glory*." This verse implies that God had prepared the vessels of his mercy before these vessels came to be. What else can this verse mean but

---

39. Flowers, *Potter's Promise*, 143.

that God planned our salvation in glory? Whatever God plans, he carries to fruition, there is nothing that he fails to do.

His own people may not receive him (John 1:11), but there will always be a faithful remnant who, despite the unbelief of the many come to faith (Rom 9:27, 11:5). Indeed, Rom 10:20 says, "I was found by those who did not seek Me; I was made manifest to those who did not ask for Me." How can you find something if you aren't even looking for it? Obviously, this implies that the thing sought out the non-seeker. In other words, God planned to bring dead sinners to life by seeking them out and finding them.

This is what Paul means in Rom 9:25–33, where he references Hos 2:21—3:1. A people who were formerly not God's people, unloved by him, shall become his beloved people. These gentiles will become the olive branches grafted into the tree of Israel in Rom 10 and 11.[40] God's first people, the Jews, were calloused and hard-hearted, and thus rejected God, despite such miracles such as the giving of the Ten Commandments, the parting of the Red Sea, and Elijah's sacrifice at Mount Carmel. On the other hand, salvation comes to the gentiles; those people groups who did not even know God, who did not have the advantages of circumcision and the oracles of God (Rom 3:1–2).

Chosen to Serve?

Another main theme in Flowers's book also related to Rom 9 is his claim that God's election is meant not for salvation, but for service. In other words, there is no distinction between "those vessels blessed with effectual salvation and those vessels cursed with reprobation," rather there is a distinction "between those vessels blessed to carry out the noble purpose of God's promise and those vessels hardened in their rebellion in order to ensure the fulfillment of the same promise."[41]

Such a position is unusual. It begs the question of why service and salvation have to be completely divorced from one another. Those whom God saves also sets into service. If you are a Christian, you will not sit idly by. The Lord will call you into service to preach, teach, go door-to-door, stack chairs, help with sound, etc.

Second Chronicles 7:16 says, "For now I have chosen and sanctified this house, that My name may be there forever; and My eyes and My heart

---

40. Robertson, *Israel of God*, 36–38.
41. Flowers, *Potter's Promise*, 139.

will be there perpetually." In this verse God not only chose the house of Solomon, but also sanctified it, so that his name, his eyes, and his heart may be there forever. Sanctification, as we have seen, is a stage in the order of salvation. One is only sanctified if one has already been chosen, called, and justified.

The prophets and the apostles were all men of God; they obviously believed in the message of salvation that they were tasked with preaching to others. It is only a saved man who can truly preach the gospel of salvation to others. A man must first experience the gospel to be able to explain it to others, it can be no other way. How can an unbeliever preach Jesus whom he doesn't know? Why would a rebellious sinner be obedient to God!? Flowers's position doesn't make sense.

When Jesus addresses the disciples at the end of Matthew's Gospel (Matt 28:18–20), he teaches them to make disciples of all nations, teaching them to keep all things that he had commanded them. Only a disciple can make another man a disciple. Jesus also tells the disciples before they are to go forth that he is with them, *even to the end of the age*. Jesus is with his disciples only. Jesus is with these disciples not only to the very end of their lives but to the end of the age. This signifies that these disciples had been regenerated and are carrying out Jesus' will.

Furthermore, let us examine John 21:15–17:

> So when they had eaten breakfast, Jesus said to Simon Peter, "Simon, son of Jonah, do you love Me more than these?" He said to Him, "Yes, Lord; You know that I love You." He said to him, "Feed My lambs." He said to him again a second time, "Simon, son of Jonah, do you love Me?" He said to Him, "Yes, Lord; You know that I love You." He said to him, "Tend My sheep." He said to him the third time, "Simon, son of Jonah, do you love Me?" Peter was grieved because He said to him the third time, "Do you love Me?" And he said to Him, "Lord, You know all things; You know that I love You." Jesus said to him, "Feed My sheep."

Previously, Peter had denied Jesus three times when they had asked him if he was Jesus' disciple. Peter had done this in unbelief. Unbelievers are those who deny Jesus and thus inherit damnation. Yet, even after Peter had regretfully denied Jesus three times, Jesus lovingly restores him, by three times tasking him to feed and tend to his sheep. If Jesus had rejected Peter for denying him three times, how would Peter have had any willpower at all to preach the gospel the way he did at Pentecost (Acts 2:14–38)? It would have been impossible. When Jesus restores a person, he also entrusts ministry to him.

A verse that has been analyzed previously is also very pertinent here: "You did not choose Me, but I chose you and appointed you that you should go and bear fruit, and that your fruit should remain, that whatever you ask the Father in My name He may give you" (John 15:16). Here Jesus clearly has chosen his disciples to go and bear fruit. Lazar counters the salvific implications of John 15:16 by referencing John 6:70: "Jesus answered them, 'Did I not choose you, the twelve, and one of you is a devil?'"[42] Here Jesus had chosen the Twelve, but one of them, namely Judas, is clearly not regenerate. Thus, Arminians argue that John 15:16 does not refer to election to salvation.

Arminians might also say that Jesus was commissioning his disciples to his ministry in this verse, so it does refer to service only, after all. Not only that, but it refers to the twelve disciples alone. Granted, but which Christian is not a disciple?

This argument does not consider the consistently Calvinist position of double predestination (or *gemini predestination*—twin predestination). John 17:12 describes the apostle Judas as the "son of perdition"—he was born unto perdition, in other words, this was Judas' fate. Of course, he was God's chosen vessel to betray Jesus, and indeed he fulfilled this task as well. Whether one is chosen for salvation or reprobation, one is also given a task to carry out. As we have seen, God chose Pharaoh in the book of Exodus to oppose him so that God could display his power and might in saving his people, Israel.

Let us examine John 15:16 in some more depth. Jesus chose his disciples so that they should bear fruit, but furthermore that their fruit *would remain*. This is not some temporary fruit coming forth from some temporary faith as in such people who receive the word with joy, but then stumble immediately when persecution arises (Matt 13:20–21).

Jesus tells us that we can recognize believers by their fruit: "Even so, every good tree bears good fruit, but a bad tree bears bad fruit. A good tree cannot bear bad fruit, nor can a bad tree bear good fruit" (Matt 7:17–18). Therefore, Jesus has chosen believers to bear fruit, good fruit, because he has chosen them for himself, to be with him forever in heaven.

Lastly, John 15:16 also implies that those whom Jesus has chosen may ask whatever they wish from the Father, in his name, they shall receive it. Although all men are God's children in a general sense, this verse implies that those whom Jesus has chosen have been adopted into God's family,

---

42. Lazar, *Chosen to Serve*, 138–40.

and thus have special access to God as their Father through Jesus. God is angry with the wicked every day (Ps 7:11), and though God does make the sun rise on the evil and on the good (Matt 5:45) as a part of the common good, God listens to his children only, and only to them does he grant their requests and desires.

The Potter's Plan

Chapter 6 of Flowers's book is only five pages long, and shall be dealt with here. It is an emotional plea to the reader to reject the God of Calvinism, whose love, Flowers alleges, is exclusive, and who cuts off children before they are even born, as opposed to his God, who loves all people inclusively.

Flowers says nothing new in this chapter. It can be reiterated that Flowers's God cuts off all babies dying in the womb from salvation since they cannot even have faith with which they need to respond to God's saving love.

Flowers even misinterprets Gen 12:3: "I will bless those who bless you, And I will curse him who curses you; And in you all the families of the earth shall be blessed." Flowers uses this verse to imply that all families of the earth shall be blessed by God. If this verse truly was all-inclusive, then it should also include those families living before Abraham. This way Flowers inadvertently cuts off all pre-Abrahamic people groups from God's salvation.

This is not the God who I would be proud of. Rather, I am proud of a God who is omniscient, almighty, all-powerful, and sovereign. God takes the initiative when man is mired in the mud of sin. When man is weak, God is strong. The God of Calvinism casts down and sets up kings and empires. When it was time for the Evil Empire to fall, it went no further than the time God had allotted for it. Nothing catches God off guard, but according to Flowers, God waits for the choices and the actions of men. God shifts and accommodates.

God is a good and gracious Potter, because he carries out his word that he said he would at the very beginning of time when he predestined all things.

"Jesus Christ is the same yesterday, today, and forever" (Heb 13:8).

— Appendix 1 —

Response to Counterarguments

> "When they heard these things they became silent; and they glorified God, saying, 'Then God has also granted to the Gentiles repentance to life.'"
>
> (Acts 11:18)

FLOWERS HAS A FINAL chapter in *The Potter's Promise* which deals with Calvinist arguments for predestination.

Why Did You Believe and Others Did Not?

The Calvinist argument as to why some come to faith while others do not is summed up by Flowers this way: *"Why did you believe the gospel, but your friend did not? Are you wiser or smarter or more spiritual or better trained or more humble?"*[1] Flowers then goes on to set up a straw man argument against Calvinism. Flowers states that the Calvinist argument presupposes God choosing people for election deterministically. He counters the alleged Calvinist argument by stating that "I believe that the cause of a choice is the chooser (or the cause of a determination is the determiner) and accept the

---

1. Flowers, *Potter's Promise*, 155. Emphasis in original.

Appendix 1

mystery associated with the functioning of that free will in making its own determinations."[2]

The fact that the human will is defined by its nature and that an indeterminate libertarian free will is meaningless has been treated in an earlier chapter. Furthermore, I think that Flowers has even misunderstood the Calvinist argument himself! Let us examine Eph 2:8–9, since it will be important for subsequent argumentation: "For by grace you have been saved through faith, *and that not of yourselves; it is the gift of God*, not of works, lest anyone should boast." However which way Flowers insistently argues for a libertarian free will and that man has the moral ability and the responsibility to choose God, this verse says very plainly that salvation is not of ourselves. This means that *the cause of salvation is outside of ourselves* (*extra nos*, a Latin phrase). There is no internal element within man that can effectively cause a man to be born again. Salvation is a gift of God; to put it more precisely, it is an *endowment* that comes with the package of salvation. It is all entirely beyond man's power to do so. That is why human intelligence, spirituality, and erudition cannot help a man. God chose us despite our abilities. Despite our sins as well.

What the Calvinist argument really means that there may be two men of equal understanding, knowledge, wisdom, personal history, and background, yet only one of them receives the gospel, the other does not. God does not choose a man for salvation because there is anything good, wonderful, attractive in him, or because he has a better understanding of things. Remember, God is so powerful that he can even save someone who cannot intellectually comprehend the gospel, or even babies in the womb.

God is so powerful that he can save even a man of less knowledge than one who has great understanding. That is why the hearts of the Pharisees were hardened, whereas men like Zakeus or the thief on the cross were saved. God chose the nation of Israel not because it was exceedingly great or powerful. How many times did God himself fight for Israel, even though they were smaller in number going against a great and mighty enemy (Exod 14:13–14)?

God elects according to his own purposes and decrees. God is not dependent upon his creation for his decrees, rather it is exactly the opposite way around. Thus, the Calvinist can truly ask his Arminians why they believed the gospel. Our intelligence, wisdom, understanding, or anything related to our human performance does not make us more or less likely to

---

2. Flowers, *Potter's Promise*, 156.

respond to the gospel. Rather, everything is contingent on God's sovereign decrees. Christians can present the gospel in every clear and winsome way, yet hearts remain cold and unresponsive. Other times they may present the gospel a bit incoherently or unclearly, yet sometimes people will respond despite these human deficits. God can use anything to turn a heart towards him. It doesn't depend on human performance.

Does the Bible really teach that God gives individuals faith first, and then they believe? Yes, it does. Acts 11:18 says "When they heard these things they became silent; and they glorified God, saying, *'Then God has also granted to the Gentiles repentance to life.'*" Jesus says in John 15:5: "I am the vine, you are the branches. He who abides in Me, and I in him, bears much fruit; for *without Me you can do nothing.*" The apostle Peter exhorts Simon the magician in the following way when he offered Peter money in order to receive the power of the Holy Spirit: "Repent therefore of this your wickedness, and *pray God if perhaps the thought of your heart may be forgiven you.* For I see that you are poisoned by bitterness and bound by iniquity" (Acts 8:22-23). This means that even if Simon repents of his wickedness, it is still up to God to grant him forgiveness. Nothing can more clearly contradict the libertarian freewill formula that man must first believe to receive salvation.

On the other hand, Flowers and Arminians of all stripes cannot answer the very question they pose. Calvinists can. Even though we appeal to God's mysterious will in election, it is a more coherent answer than the Arminian resort to uninfluenced, sovereign free will. As Peterson and Williams note, if man cannot be brought or even influenced by grace to accept Christ, neither can he be influenced by sin in either direction. If man's will is indeterminate to the point of complete inaction, Arminians truly cannot explain why one man believes and the other man does not.[3]

Calvinists Ultimately Appeal to the Same Mystery

Flowers argues that Calvinists cannot use the argument which says that man cannot choose God, precisely because his fallen nature prohibits him from doing so. Flowers asks, what about the first sin, then? If man in his unfallen state could make a choice to fall into sin, then does this not mean that his nature is mutable? The Calvinist has no rational answer as to why

---

3. Peterson and Williams, *Why I Am Not*, 130.

Adam or Lucifer chose to rebel. Why deny libertarian free will then? Or that man's nature could not be libertarian free as well?

The argument may sound reasonable, but it is not biblical. As to why Adam chose to sin when he was sinless is a mystery. Flowers may accuse Calvinists of appealing to mystery without warrant, but there is one thing that we can know: if Adam in his sinless state chose to sin, then why does Flowers have the courage to then claim that man in his fallen state can be morally stronger than Adam in his unfallen state and choose to do good? The Bible does say, "Who can bring a clean thing out of an unclean? No one!" (Job 14:4). In Jer 13:23 we read, "Can the Ethiopian change his skin or the leopard its spots? Then may you also do good who are accustomed to do evil." The Bible does say that we cannot change our fallen human nature. So, no, man's nature is not libertarian free as Flowers might suggest. When man fell into sin, it was a one-way door, and he was cemented in the ways of sin and misery. There is no way out of sin. Man died spiritually and cannot spark faith in himself. Man cannot save himself. Man in his rebellion cannot even want to save himself.

Better by Choice or Divine Decree?

Flowers makes the surprising claim that Calvinists say that the reason they chose to believe in Christ is because God made them morally better than the rest of humanity. The traditionalist, on the other hand, would say that everyone has the same God-given moral capacity to believe in Christ, and no one is made morally "better" by God. Flowers accuses Calvinists of spiritual arrogance for claiming that they are morally better because God made them that way.[4]

Flowers's argumentation is completely misguided. What does Rom 12:3 say? *"For I say, through the grace given to me, to everyone who is among you, not to think of himself more highly than he ought to think, but to think soberly, as God has dealt to each one a measure of faith."* It is precisely the Calvinist position, as stated earlier in this chapter, that God chose people *not because of anything in them*. First Corinthians 4:7 says, "For who makes you differ from another? *And what do you have that you did not receive? Now if you did indeed receive it, why do you boast as if you had not received it?*" Calvinism puts great stress on the fact that we have received everything from God, *literally everything*! Our bodies, our minds, our hair,

---

4. Flowers, *Potter's Promise*, 160.

our skin, our bones, blood, our job, our family, our possessions, and, yes, even, and most importantly of all, our salvation.

Calvin understood this very well, and this is what he writes in the Institutes linking election with humility: "We shall never feel persuaded as we ought that our salvation flows from the free mercy of God as its fountain, until we are made acquainted with his eternal election, the grace of God being illustrated by the contrast, viz., that he does not adopt all promiscuously to the hope of salvation, but gives to some what he denies to others. It is plain how greatly ignorance of this principle detracts from the glory of God, and impairs true humility."[5]

The statement that "we chose God because God made us morally better than everyone else" is completely false and misrepresents the Calvinist concept of salvation. According to the Calvinist system of salvation, as described in the *ordo salutis*, first a man is regenerated by the Holy Spirit, and is then enabled to choose God. This is because by nature, man is spiritually dead and in rebellion against his Creator.

Calvinists know very well that their rebirth, their spirituality, their intellect, wisdom, etc. are not of themselves, but rather a gift of God. They have not themselves to praise but God alone. "He who glories, let him glory in the Lord" (1 Cor 1:31). Why would one claim that he has salvation because he was chosen if it is God who chooses? This is something characteristic of freewill theology, not Calvinism. Furthermore, the moral qualities of a man are not what is important in salvation, rather, the work of Christ. Flowers is so focused on importing human effort into salvation that he views salvation as a moral effort on man's part.

Going back to Eph 2:9, quoted earlier, we are not saved by our works, lest we should boast. Flowers is the one emphasizing man's moral capacity, his ability to do something to achieve his own salvation. According to libertarian freewill theology, minus a choice on the part of man for Christ means that person is lost forever. It is incumbent upon man to respond to God's offer of salvation. Flowers inadvertently reveals his works-based mentality by writing: "Whether one believes because they were sovereignly made to do so or simply given the ability to do so freely does not change the fact that believers are *doing* something 'morally better.'"[6] Therefore it is the provisionist who would want to boast in his insight that allegedly gets him from the state of the despair and misery of sin into the kingdom of God.

---

5. Calvin, *Institutes*, 202.
6. Flowers, *Potter's Promise*, 160.

Appendix 1

A Decision Does Not Merit Salvation

An important issue in the debate on free will and Calvinism is whether a libertarian free choice merits salvation. Flowers vigorously denies this claim. He rightfully claims that asking for forgiveness does not merit being forgiven; we are forgiven only because God is gracious. He mentions that the prodigal son in Luke 15 did not merit salvation because he humbly returned home. Flowers writes, "God gives grace to the humble not because a humble response deserves salvation, but because He is gracious."[7] Salvation belongs to the Lord, but Flowers still holds out by claiming that responsibility to repent is also from him. Flowers claims that there are no biblical grounds for saying that man does not have the moral ability to respond to God's gracious appeals to repent.

Despite Flowers's appeals, salvation is either entirely of Christ, or it is works-based. If one must do even one deed, think one thought or make one choice for salvation, then the basis of salvation rests on man's work. Arminians and provisionists simply cannot get past the idea, originating from Pelagius, that if God commands men to have faith and obedience to him in Scripture, then that also means that they have the capability of doing so. In this sense there is only a *quantitative* difference between the Pelagian and the Arminian; their views on salvation are *qualitatively* the same. In other words, Pelagianism, semi-Pelagianism, Arminianism, and provisionism all fall essentially into the same category.

According to Ian Hamilton, "faith is trust in another; faith is the acknowledgment that all our hope lies outside of ourselves." We bring nothing to the judgment seat of God that can save us. There is nothing we can do to buy or to deserve salvation, that is why salvation is a gift. We don't decide what kind of gifts we receive. If we could do anything to receive salvation, it would be a reward, not a gift.[8] Romans 4:4 says, "Now to him who works, the wages are not counted as grace but as debt."

It would be worth reviewing the views on salvation of Jakob Hermanszoon (Jacobus Arminius, 1560–1609), the founder of Arminian theology. Arminius cites Rom 10:5, "*do* this, and live," and then interprets it by saying, "If man is deprived of any of these qualifications, such admonitions as these cannot possibly be effective in exciting him to obedience."[9] Therefore

---

7. Flowers, *Potter's Promise*, 161–62.
8. Hamilton, *Salvation*, 66–67.
9. Arminius, *Arminius Speaks*, 42.

it is no surprise that he continues to interpret salvation as belonging to those "who *believe* in the name of Jesus Christ" (John 1:12), or that salvation is "*the reward of obedience*" (Matt 5:12), or that it is the "*labor* of love" (Heb 6:10), and that we must *fight* the good fight and *run* well (Rev 2:10; 2 Tim 4:7–8), and that we must *work* our own salvation (Phil 2:12).[10]

Note the action verbs in Arminius' writings: do, believe, labor, fight, run, work. Even if believing in Christ for salvation is expressed in thought, word, or any kind of deed, it is still something *within* a man. Arminius interprets these verses as *man's active response* to God. But this theology is in stark contradistinction with Eph 2:8: "For by grace you have been saved through faith, and that *not of yourselves*; it is the *gift* of God."

Olson brings a similar example of a starving college student without any money. A kindly professor has compassion on him and writes him a check for $1000. The student has only to *take* the check to his bank, *endorse* it, and *deposit* the check. This common Arminian analogy of salvation (the professor symbolizing the gracious God and the college student the needy sinner) is replete with action verbs: take, endorse, deposit.[11] Arminius himself also emphasized human action to attain salvation: to do this and live (Rom 10:5), or to believe in the name of Jesus Christ (John 1:12), to fight the good fight and run well (Rev 2:10; 2 Tim 4:7–8).[12] Free will theology cannot avoid emphasizing man's initiative.

The prodigal son is the last in a set of three parables of God seeking the lost in Luke 15, as mentioned earlier. The previous two parables of the lost sheep and the lost coin are related to it. God does take initiative in salvation, in seeking out the lost coin and the lost sheep. Man has no power over this. However, man is still responsible to turn from his sin and repent, just as the prodigal son came to his senses and makes an effort to stand up and return to his father's house. These two aspects of salvation go together; Calvinism does not deny man's responsibility, but rather weaves it together with God's initiative.

The Bible on Our Responsibility

Flowers brings eighteen verses, all of which have to do with God showing mercy to the humble. These verses are 2 Kgs 22:19; 2 Chr 12:7, 12; Ps 18:27;

10. Arminius, *Arminius Speaks*, 44, 48.
11. Olson, *Against Calvinism*, 170.
12. Arminius, *Arminius Speaks*, 42, 44, 28.

Appendix 1

25:9; 147:6; Prov 3:34; Isa 66:2; Zeph 2:3; Matt 5:3; 18:4; 23:12; Luke 1:52; 14:11; 18:14; 1 Pet 5:5–6; and Jas 4:6, 10. Flowers acknowledges that God shows mercy to whomever he wants to show mercy, even with a reference to Rom 9:15. But he then adds that it is no secret as to whom God wishes to show mercy. He also states that we have a responsibility to humble ourselves for us to be accepted by God so that he would choose us.[13]

This statement does not make sense, and merely illustrates Flowers's works-based mentality, inherited from Arminius as described in the previous section. What Flowers is saying is that man must first humble himself before he has a chance of salvation. Humbling oneself is an action that man must perform. Man initiates his own salvation, not God, who takes a mere passive role.

Is man truly humble? Can he really change his own heart to be acceptable and pleasing to God? What was said about the state of man's heart applies here. Man can never truly humble himself towards God, apart from a work of regeneration in the heart of man by the Holy Spirit and the renewal of his mind (Rom 12:1–2). "The heart is deceitful above all things, and desperately wicked; who can know it?" (Jer 17:9)

Calvinists fully accept all eighteen verses that Flowers lists. But they also fully understand the total depravity of man and the inability to change himself. Man is totally dependent upon God giving him a new heart and making him a new creation: "Therefore, if anyone is in Christ, he is a new creation; old things have passed away; behold, all things have become new." (2 Cor 5:17). Just as man cannot give birth to himself, so much less can he re-create himself. This would be nothing less than self-regeneration, a concept foreign to Scripture.

What Flowers is talking about is completely impossible for man to accomplish, yet it can still be done by God's grace. Let us read about Jesus' dialogue with the rich man in Mark 10:17–22. Jesus tells the man that he must give up all his wealth and follow him so that he can be saved. This the rich young man could not do. He trusts too much in his own riches. For him, money is his savior. He trusts that with money he can solve any problem. The rich young man puts his trust in something other than God.

If we are honest with ourselves, we are all like this. We are all putting our trust in something other than God, be it money, power, influence, or any other thing which identifies us. By ourselves we simply cannot let go of our lives and humble ourselves before God as Flowers demands. Flowers is

---

13. Flowers, *Potter's Promise*, 167–68.

trying to turn on a flashlight which doesn't have any batteries in it. Second Corinthians 3:17 says, "Now the Lord is the Spirit; and where the Spirit of the Lord is, there is liberty." If a sinner is only free if he has the Spirit, how can man choose the Spirit if he does not yet have the Spirit to make him free?

Flowers demands that fallen, depraved sinners do something spiritual, when they themselves lack the Holy Spirit. First Corinthians 2:14 says this very well: "*But the natural man does not receive the things of the Spirit of God, for they are foolishness to him; nor can he know them, because they are spiritually discerned.*" Romans 8:5–8 makes this even more clear: "*For those who live according to the flesh set their minds on the things of the flesh, but those who live according to the Spirit, the things of the Spirit. For to be carnally minded is death, but to be spiritually minded is life and peace. Because the carnal mind is enmity against God; for it is not subject to the law of God, nor indeed can be. So then, those who are in the flesh cannot please God.*" Those who are in the flesh do not live according to the Spirit, and thus cannot please God in any way, even by choosing God according to their libertarian free will.

So how can someone get saved? Let us read further in Mark 10, verses 25–27: "It is easier for a camel to go through the eye of a needle than for a rich man to enter the kingdom of God. And they were greatly astonished, saying among themselves, 'Who then can be saved?' But Jesus looked at them and said, '*With men it is impossible, but not with God; for with God all things are possible.*'"

Only by a work of God's Holy Spirit can we be saved. That is how far we are from God. But, once we are saved, we are continually sanctified and conformed to the image of Christ (Rom 8:29). This is the process of sanctification that starts the moment we are regenerated and saved. Question 35 in the Westminster Shorter Catechism asks, "What is sanctification?" To which the response is: "Sanctification is the work of God's free grace, whereby we are renewed in the whole man after the image of God, and are enabled more and more to die unto sin, and live unto righteousness."[14] Second Thessalonians 2:13 states, "God from the beginning chose you for salvation through *sanctification by the Spirit* and belief in the truth." Flowers conflates sanctification with justification, which is the self-same error that Roman Catholicism makes when talking about salvation. The fruits of sanctification, such as humility, are a work of the Holy Spirit within a born-again believer. In other words, those who are humble, or meek, the merciful and the pure in

---

14. Smith, *Systematic Theology*, 54.

heart can only be people who have already been born again. For example, Matt 5:5 says that "blessed are the meek, for they shall inherit the earth." These are the meek, who have become meek in character by the work of the Holy Spirit, and only they shall inherit the earth, as part of their salvation.

Should Implies Could

It is as if Pelagius himself is speaking through Flowers's pen from over a thousand years ago. Flowers here repeats the Pelagian argument that should implies could—if God issues a command to man, man should be able to carry out God's command, otherwise why should he be responsible for not doing so? Flowers takes this as clear, common sense. But just because it is logical humanly speaking, is it theo-logical as well?

Note that *could* implies man's *power* to do something, not something God has done for us. Flowers is stuck in a works-based mindset. Again, we must reiterate here that man has the *natural* ability to repent and respond to God but lacks the *moral* ability to do so. If man has rebelled against God's laws, he is definitely in no mind to be obedient to God. Pink rightly argues that even though man has lost his moral ability to repent, God has not lost his right to call man to responsibility. Pink writes: "The creature's impotence does not cancel his obligation. A drunken servant is a servant still, and it is contrary to all sound reasoning that argue that his master loses his rights through his servant's defaults."[15]

Flowers illustrates his views on man's ability with the following analogy: Flowers played a family activity with his children where he would stand at the top of a flight of stairs, with his three children at the bottom. The rules of the game were that the children would have to get to the top of the stairs without stepping on the stairs, or even using the railing, or even the wall. After looking at each other in bewilderment, they broke down, utterly confused—the task was utterly impossible!

Obviously, Flowers wants to illustrate climbing the stairs as analogous to human performance in achieving salvation by works. The children would have to walk up the stairs, grasp the railing, or do something to physically translocate themselves from the bottom of the stairs to the top. Flowers denies works-based salvation, yet he believes that man can respond somehow to God. That is why commends his children when they finally ask for his help to carry them up the flight of stairs to the top. In Flowers's system,

15. Pink, *Sovereignty of God*, 155.

Response to Counterarguments

when the children ask him to carry them up the stairs is analogous to asking Jesus into your heart or choosing Christ. Flowers then critiques the Calvinist system which he claims doesn't even allow for man to respond to God.[16]

Incidentally, the picture of Flowers carrying his children up the flight of stairs is quite different from the picture on Flowers's later book, *God's Provision for All*, featuring a man climbing up the hill, only to be helped up at the very top by another man. It appears that Flowers's worldview is progressing steadily away from God's grace towards man's ability and action over time.

This is a clever analogy on Flowers's part, but it has already been formulated previously in other ways. Another picture that Arminians use is that of a severely ill man. The man is so severely ill that he is bedridden and cannot even move. He cannot even move a muscle. He is an inch away from death. However, there is a physician with a life-saving medication that can heal the man and restore him to life. The man's friends arrange for the physician to come and offer the man the life-saving medication. All that the man must do is open his lips and receive the medication, and he will fully recover.[17]

These analogies break down because they inaccurately depict man's condition. Flowers would have us believe that our city streets are teeming with people wondering how to get to God. It is as if they spend every passing moment trying to figure out how to be saved. Rather, people are trying to figure out how to run away from and escape God. Others deny God altogether so that they can live however which way they please. Romans 3:11–12 says, "There is none who understands; *there is none who seeks after God*. They have all turned aside; they have together become unprofitable; there is none who does good, no, not one." Reformulating Flowers's analogy with the flight of stairs, the children at the bottom of the stairs would be more accurately portrayed as either ignoring their father, fighting each other, or running outside to play instead of doing their chores.

This is why Reformed theologians such as John Calvin and Jonathan Edwards all described humanity as being at enmity with God, inventing idols, and heresies so as to avoid having to repent and conform to God's ways. The human heart proudly exalts itself against God. People hate God

---

16. Flowers, *Potter's Promise*, 171–73.

17. This concept goes back to John Cassian (360–435), the abbot of the monastery of Massilia in France, who was arguably the first semi-Pelagian. Cassian affirmed that man's will is not enslaved to sin, but only weakened: *infirmitas liberi arbitrii*. Furthermore, he believed that Adam's sin was only a hereditary disease, not spiritual death (Sproul, *Willing to Believe*, 70–72).

Appendix 1

and love themselves. They are blind to their own sin, which is the necessary first thing they need to remedy their corruption.[18]

But how do we resolve Flowers's dilemma? Does should really imply could? Is it a necessary inference that if God commands us to do something, then we truly have the power to do so? Let's read Gal 3:23–25, which resolves the dilemma: "But before faith came, we were kept under guard by the law, kept for the faith which would afterward be revealed. *Therefore the law was our tutor to bring us to Christ, that we might be justified by faith.* But after faith has come, we are no longer under a tutor." Augustine, Calvin, and Luther have all rightly asserted that the law merely tells us *what we ought to do*. It does not address the question of *whether we actually have the power to do so*. The law is an expression of the will of God.[19] Augustine described the relationship between law and human will this way: "O, man! Learn from the precept what you ought to do; learn from correction, that it is your own fault *you have not the power*; and learn in prayer, whence it is that you may receive the power."[20]

Similarly, R. C. Sproul explains that John 3:16 indeed promises that whosoever believes will not perish but will have eternal life. Again, it is a possible inference that if someone chooses to believe in Christ, then he will be saved, but it is not a necessary inference. John 3:16 speaks only about what happens to someone when they believe, but it doesn't say anything about who will or can believe.[21] Interestingly, Gottschalk points out in verse 18, that "but he who does not believe *is condemned already*," meaning that condemnation came first to the reprobate, who will never come to faith.[22] Similarly, in Rom 5:10 we read, "For if *when we were enemies* we were reconciled to God through the death of His Son, much more, having been reconciled, we shall be saved by His life." "When we were enemies" denotes the past tense, which could only mean that those who believe had already been chosen for reconciliation with God. See also John 10:26, Prov 16:4, and Rom 9:22.

Of Pelagianism, semi-Pelagianism, Arminianism, and Provisionism, Pelagianism is the most consistent. Salvation really is an all or nothing game. It is either all of grace, or all of keeping the law. If should really does

18. Davidson, "Unholy Hate," 645–51.
19. Luther, *Bondage of the Will*.
20. From Augustine's *De Correptione et Gratia*, cited in Calvin, *Institutes*, 301.
21. Sproul, *Willing to Believe*, 100–101.
22. Genke and Gumerlock, *Gottschalk*, 71–72.

Response to Counterarguments

imply could, and if man is truly capable of responding to God and making a freewill decision for Christ, then it must follow that man can do all things pleasing to God. Why stop at this one thing? Why not adopt the full-blown Pelagian system? If man can do one thing, he can do another thing. After all, he is capable of keeping all of the law.

> The lot is cast into the lap, but *its every decision is from the Lord.* (Prov 16:33).

Flowers takes man's innate capability of responding to God a step further. In his later book, *God's Provision for All*, he claims that the natural man is capable of freely responding to divine revelation, and that no extra grace is necessary for man to understand what God is telling him. According to Flowers, "Mankind has been created by God with the basic capability to hear, understand and respond to clearly revealed truth."[23]

The problem is that Flowers completely misunderstands and misinterprets the nature of divine revelation. Adam may have been able to understand God when he spoke to him, but after the fall, all of man's faculties are affected by sin. Apparently, Flowers denies the effects of original sin in the human mind. It is not that God's grace through unmediated revelation is insufficient, rather, God abounds in grace, so much so that by his Holy Spirit God opens our minds to understand divine truth, something that Jesus did to the two disciples on the way to Emmaus (Luke 24:13–35).

After the resurrection, Jesus meets two disciples on the way to Emmaus. After inquiring of what they were talking about, namely, the crucifixion of Jesus on the cross, Jesus explains to them the prophecies of Christ in the Old Testament starting from Moses and the prophets (verses 25–27). It was only a while later when they had gotten off the road and were having dinner that these two disciples even understood what Jesus was talking to them. Even then, their eyes had to be opened to understand the Scriptures they already knew (verse 25).

In the very next part of Scripture (Luke 24:36–49) Jesus appears to his fearful disciples, huddling together in a room after the Resurrection. They are astonished when he appears in their midst, demonstrating to them that he had indeed risen from the dead. Verses 44–45 then say, "Then He said to them, 'These are the words which I spoke to you while I was still with you, that all things must be fulfilled which were written in the Law of Moses and the Prophets and the Psalms concerning Me.' *And He opened*

---

23. Flowers, *God's Provision*, 65–66.

Appendix 1

their understanding, that they might comprehend the Scriptures." Here are the disciples, the very men who had been with Jesus for three years and listened to his every word, even those which were not written down in the Bible, yet time and time again, they were hard of understanding, to the point that Jesus had to scold them several times for their lack of understanding. If Jesus' own disciples, who had been with him for three years, did not understand the Lord, why would people in a different culture, removed in time and geography, understand him any better than they did? Not only that, even after the disciples had seen Jesus resurrected with their own eyes, Jesus had to open their minds to understand the fulfilled Scripture.

And even when the disciples did get things right, then it was God himself who implanted the thought into their minds. In Matt 16 Jesus asks his disciples who they think that he is. Simon Peter answered by saying that Jesus was Christ, the Son of the living God. In verse 17, Jesus responds to Peter by saying: "Blessed are you, Simon Bar-Jonah, for flesh and blood has not revealed this to you, *but My Father who is in heaven.*"

Furthermore, when Jesus tells the multitude the parable of the sower in Mark 4:9–12, he declares to them that "he who has ears to hear, let him hear!" In other words, the one who has been given understanding (because he is elect) is the one who is able to not only hear but comprehend the parable. According to verses 10–12:

> But when He was alone, those around Him with the twelve asked Him about the parable. And He said to them, "To you it has been given to know the mystery of the kingdom of God; but to those who are outside, all things come in parables, so that *'seeing they may see and not perceive, and hearing they may hear and not understand; lest they should turn, and their sins be forgiven them.'*"

Clearly, to some people it has been given to God to understand his mysteries, but from others it was withheld, even with the intent that they would not understand so that they may repent. This passage clearly demonstrates God's reprobating certain people.

These verses clearly contradict Flowers's teaching which is overly optimistic towards human understanding. It is as if Flowers is leaving only a small role for the Holy Spirit to play in transmitting divine truth to men. John 6:63 says, "It is the Spirit who gives life; *the flesh profits nothing.* The words that I speak to you are spirit, and they are life." The next two verses say, "'But there are some of you who do not believe.' For Jesus knew from the beginning who they were who did not believe, and who would betray

Response to Counterarguments

Him. And He said, 'Therefore I have said to you that no one can come to Me unless it has been granted to him by My Father.'"[24]

Romans 8:5 says, "*For those who live according to the flesh set their minds on the things of the flesh,* but those who live according to the Spirit, the things of the Spirit." First Corinthians 2:14 says, "But the natural man does not receive the things of the Spirit of God, for they are foolishness to him; nor can he know them, because they are spiritually discerned."

Calvin argues that we must first come to the point where we realize that we cannot do anything for ourselves but must rely on God entirely for everything. It was Luther's long, hard struggle with keeping the law out of self-righteousness before he realized that the righteous shall live by faith (Rom 1:17). Jesus says in John 15:5, that "without me you can do nothing." But Jesus also says that "with men this is impossible, but with God all things are possible" (Matt 19:26). Clearly, if we let free will seep into the church, it leads to self-righteousness and works-based salvation.

Lastly, Flowers surprisingly argues against original sin, the doctrine that all men are born sinners because of Adam's sin. Flowers writes, "Scripture never once says that we will perish because of Adam's sin."[25] This is only the outworking of Flowers's flawed theology. The Holy Spirit has always taught the doctrine of original sin all throughout history, and Scripture refutes Flowers's denial. Let us look at several verses from Romans 5:

- "Nevertheless death reigned from Adam to Moses, *even over those who had not sinned according to the likeness of the transgression of Adam,* who is a type of Him who was to come" (verse 14).

- "*For if by the one man's offense death reigned through the one,* much more those who receive abundance of grace and of the gift of righteousness will reign in life through the One, Jesus Christ" (verse 17).

- "For as by one man's disobedience many were made sinners, so also by one Man's obedience many will be made righteous" (verse 19).

All men shall stand without excuse before their Creator on judgement day (Rom 1:20). Flowers's book ends with a fictional dialogue between a reprobate and God (the Judge):

> *Judge:* "Why did you remain in unbelief?"

---

24. Apparently, this was a hard saying for Jesus' audience to hear, and so in verse 66 it says that many of his disciples went away and walked with him no more.

25. Flowers, *Potter's Promise*, 175.

Appendix 1

Reprobate: "I was born hated and rejected by my God who sealed me in unbelief from the time I was born until the time I died due to the sin of another [Adam]."[26]

We have to stress that this indeed is a fictional dialogue, which never has, and never will take place, because of what the Bible says. As I have argued in this book, man is predestined for either heaven or hell, but this does not detract from his responsibility. The doctrine of concurrence, as detailed in previous pages, proves this. It was God's foreordained plan to crucify his own Son: "Him, being delivered by the determined purpose and foreknowledge of God, you have taken by lawless hands, have crucified, and put to death" (Acts 2:23). Judas, the son of perdition (John 17:12), who took part in this crucifixion by betraying Jesus to the Jews, shall acknowledge his sin before Almighty God on judgement day: "I have sinned by betraying innocent blood" (Matt 27:4).

God calls to all, but are you chosen? If so, respond now to God, today while there is still time. *"He who has ears to hear, let him hear!"* (Mark 4:9).

> Just as He chose us in Him before the foundation of the world, that we should be holy and without blame before Him in love. (Eph 1:4)

---

26. Flowers, *Potter's Promise*, 175.

Summary
Clearing Up Common Misunderstandings of Calvinism

"Blessed are you when they revile and persecute you, and say all kinds of evil against you falsely for My sake. Rejoice and be exceedingly glad, for great is your reward in heaven, for so they persecuted the prophets who were before you."

(MATT 5:11–12)

Transcendence and Immanence

DURING CHURCH HISTORY, UNORTHODOX doctrines have arisen many times due to an imbalance between two elements of God's character: God's transcendence and his immanence. God's transcendence involves God's incomprehensibility, his distance, and his "otherness" compared to human beings. This involves God's sovereignty, his absolute lordship over all of creation, and election. God's immanence, on the other hand, describes how close God can come to human beings. God is distant, but he is also close, and knows us intimately. He knows all our thoughts. In him we live and move and have our being (Acts 17:28). He is here with us by the Holy Spirit (John 15:26). God came so close to us that he even became one of us in his Son, Jesus Christ. As a man Jesus was beaten, tortured, and crucified for our sakes. It is extremely important to stress that God is both transcendent, but also immanent at the same time.

Summary

Very often Arminians, such as Flowers, are not debating with what can really considered to be Calvinist arguments. Pictures of the alleged Calvinist God as a puppet-master or a totalitarian despotic ruler are mere caricatures of Calvinism. Calvinism itself can fall into the error or hyper-Calvinism, which indeed overemphasizes God's transcendence, to the point that some hyper-Calvinists do not care much about evangelizing. They argue that if God really wants to save someone because he is God's elect, then God will save him. It is this distorted hyper-Calvinistic caricature of Calvinism that most Arminians so ardently attack. It's all just a straw man that Arminians want to take down.

If hyper-Calvinism tends towards a transcendental imbalance on one end, then there must also exist an immanence imbalance. This position is Arminianism/provisionism/freewill theology. Try as they might, Arminians simply cannot get past Eph 2:8: "For by grace you have been saved through faith, and that *not of yourselves*." Salvation is entirely outside of human capability. If we are spiritually dead, then we simply cannot respond to God. Yet Arminians demand that man's sacrosanct free will in deciding his own eternal fate cannot be impinged upon. The bottom line is that the Arminian viewpoint is based on at least one work of man. Namely his unimpeded freewill choice in choosing Christ. There is only a quantitative difference between the Arminian and the Roman Catholic position.

Calvinism strikes the balance between the immanent and the transcendent character of God (figure 8). True, historical, orthodox Calvinism has never, ever denied man's responsibility in repenting and having faith in God. Yet, God is sovereign and determines all things at the same time. The discussion in chapter 3 on concurrence makes this abundantly clear. Verses such as Ps 37:23, Prov 16:1, 21:1, John 6:37, and Phil 2:12–13 present this mystery. All these verses describe man's ability, and the imperative to repent, but at the same time they stress God's sovereignty and election as the backdrop to man's actions.

God calls men to repent, therefore they are left without excuse (Acts 17:30–31). Disobedience to God's imperative command to repent puts all responsibility on man. As such, since many men do not repent, God is justified in sending them to hell to suffer forever. God is not wicked for punishing humans for their sins, because this is what we really all deserve. Rather, God is loving because he graciously chose to save a portion of humanity, the elect, for salvation (Eph 1:4).

Summary

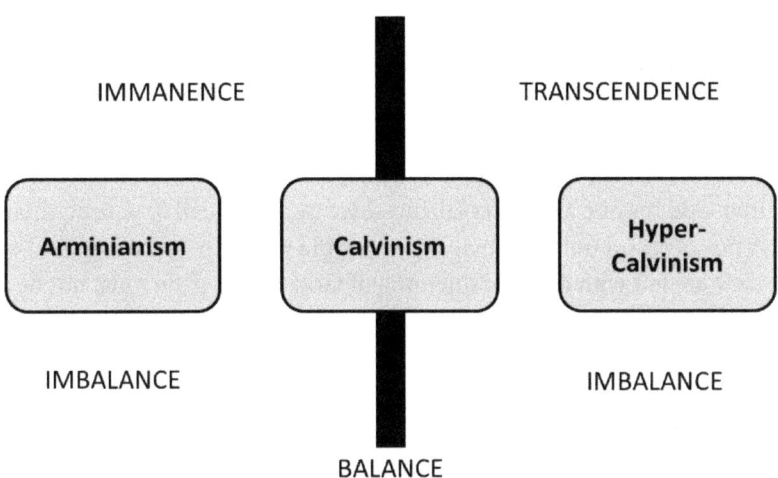

God never, ever was forced to enter a covenant of redemption with his Son to save us from our sins. Since we all sinned in Adam, we must also die in sin. It is purely God's unmerited and unmeritable grace that Jesus would die for even one sin of one man. All this, and God completely preserves his loving character. If Arminians argue that God cannot force salvation on unwilling humans, they must be charitable towards God and not force God to show his love the way they want him to. But, since God is so truly loving, that is why he sent Jesus to us. God is loving beyond all measure!

God's Love, Power, and Justice

At the center of the Calvinist/Arminian debate are three crucial concepts: God's love, God's power (sovereignty), and God's justice.[1] God is a God of love and in him there is no malice or wickedness. This is akin to God's immanence, described earlier. But God is also all-powerful, and not only can do all things, but has also determined all things. This corresponds to God's transcendence. The third point has to do with the existence of evil (both natural evil, such as diseases and earthquakes, and moral evil, such as murder or theft) in the world, a question that has plagued thinkers all throughout human history. God is not just loving and all-powerful, but he is also just. He hates sin, and must punish it, since it is contrary to his

1. Pinnock, *Grace of God*, 31–33.

Summary

will. God's hatred and punishment of sin is not unloving, because sin goes contrary to God's good character.

Tensions arise when we consider God's loving nature. If God is loving, then why is there evil in the world at all? Since there is evil, is God not powerful enough to deal with all this evil? God must be able to deal with evil since he is just. Some people (a small minority, such as some atheists) say that God may be all-powerful, but since he allows evil to persist, then he must not be good but even evil. Most people recoil from calling God evil, but they are left with another dilemma: if God is loving, he must not be all-powerful, because if he was, he would deal with sin and evil. This relegates God to a kind of kindly Santa Claus, who is well-wishing, but unable to direct the affairs of the universe.

This kind of thinking also leads people to materialistic evolution. God may be good, but if he is not powerful enough to deal with sin, *then he really isn't God*. Let this sink in for a while: atheists correctly understand that if God is not all-powerful (an incommunicable attribute if God that cannot be compromised with), then he really isn't God; therefore, God doesn't exist. But since we are here, we must have gotten here by the movement of matter upon itself, which is materialistic evolution.[2]

If we consider this point hard enough, we can discern that this kind of God corresponds to the god of the dualistic Manichaean kind, where Arminianism leads to. This god loves all men the same and wants to save each and every single person in the world, but yet is incapable of convincing them of his love. Again, this is because Arminianism overemphasizes God's immanence, and is thus imbalanced and undergoes tension.

However, in Calvinism, God is all-powerful and sovereign, since whatever he foreordains comes to pass without fail, without question, and without delay, at its appropriate and appointed time. For example, the prophet Elisha prophesied that within a day the famine that had struck Israel would cease and food prices would come back to normal (2 Kgs 7:1–2), which happened exactly as Elisha prophesied (2 Kgs 7:18–20).

Since God is also all-powerful, he also has evil under his control. Whatever he commands the great adversary, Satan, to do, he must do. Satan cannot concoct or devise any scheme or plan to undo God's sovereign will. Evil will never triumph over good. We must see that God, in his

---

2. Also consider that if God is not sovereign over man's will, then that means there is an element in the universe over which God has no control over. Thus, God is not sovereign. If God is not sovereign, neither is he all-powerful, and as such he really isn't God. In this manner also the consequence of Arminianism is atheism . . .

sovereignty, restricts evil and does not allow it to come into full blossom, *thus God is also good!*

God may allow evil (see the numerous examples in the appendix), such as bringing calamities, bringing foreign armies upon nations to chastise them, or allowing people to fall into illness, to wake them up from their sins. Yet, in a mysterious manner, God is not the author of sin, only man is responsible for it. God may allow evil in his grand, overarching plan, and can bring good out of evil (Gen 50:20). We may not see all the details of God's overarching plans carried out in world history, but we must accept that God is good, and have faith in him.

Prayer and Evangelization

One may often hear the charge against Calvinists that if God is absolutely sovereign, and we have no say in our salvation, then why evangelize at all? Also, why pray at all, if God fulfills his will without human cooperation of any kind? Calvinists are sometimes portrayed as hardhearted, unloving, cold people who do not care for their neighbors.

The answer is much simpler than the antagonists of Calvinism may even think. When God sends forth his word, he uses tools: prophets in the Old Testament, apostles, evangelists, teachers, and pastors in the New Testament era. Jesus commands his church in Matt 28:19–20 to teach the nations: "Go therefore and make disciples of all the nations, baptizing them in the name of the Father and of the Son and of the Holy Spirit, teaching them to observe all things that I have commanded you; and lo, I am with you always, even to the end of the age. Amen." In this passage of Scripture, we have a command from God to spread the good news to all men. If we do not obey this command, then we are in sin. Furthermore, if we persistently do not spread the gospel, we are continuing in sin, and these are signs of an unregenerate heart. If you do not have God's love, then you have nothing to give to others. However, if your cup is filled with the love of God, you cannot help but share it with others. Here the bottom line is love: if you love God and reflect Jesus, others will see this in your life and hear it from your lips.

And indeed, some of the greatest missionaries, such as William Carey, David Livingstone, Adinoram Judson, and J. Hudson Taylor who spread the gospel to people in Africa, India, and China with such great missionary

Summary

zeal, were Calvinists.[3] Calvinists love others so much that they would travel to faraway lands and risk their lives to preach about the love of God that dwells in them.

The author could also mention his experience in the ministry starting only three years after he became Christian. He was involved very early on in the creation science ministry and helped establish a creation science group in Hungary in 2001. As an elder at a Presbyterian church, he also regularly takes part in prayer evangelization on the streets of Whittier, California, and also oversees door to door ministry at his church.

There do exist some Reformed churches that are "hyper-Calvinist," to the point that they truly do not have any program for evangelization. Their underlying thought is that "if God wants to save my neighbor, then he has the power to do so, without my help." Some hyper-Calvinist churches that believe this exist in Switzerland and France, but their numbers are in decline. To presume that Calvinists have no incentive to evangelize is another aberrant overemphasis of God's transcendence. It bears repeating that God is both transcendent but also immanent. God elects, but he uses tools to carry forth his word.

If the evangelistic mindset can err too heavily on the transcendent side, it can also err on the immanent side as well. This leads to aberrant methods and attitudes towards evangelism on the Arminian side. Seeker friendly-ism has watered down the gospel to the point that in some churches the gospel is not preached, lest one nonbeliever be offended. If the gospel is watered down, or if other "offensive" doctrines are avoided, then Arminians run the risk of not proclaiming the entire testimony of Scripture. We must keep in mind that if we offend, we offend with the gospel. These churches would do well to keep such verses in mind, such as Prov 27:6: "Faithful are the wounds of a friend, but the kisses of an enemy are deceitful." A de-emphasis of God's holiness and sanctification has led to the spread of immorality in churches, and church discipline is also widely not practiced, in some places it is not even heard of, and even scorned.[4] Yet, it is a mark of the true church.

As a corollary, some may ask, if God has already foreordained all things that come to pass, then why pray at all? How can my prayer change anything if everything has been determined by God? As previously stated, God uses us as his tools to achieve his goals, and these include our prayers.

---

3. González, *Story of Christianity*, 306–13.
4. Laney, *Guide to Church Discipline*, 11–26.

Summary

Although God has transcendentally foreordained all events, from a human perspective, we live in a dynamic world. We can only see a few steps ahead of ourselves, whereas God sees everything from eternity past to eternity future. God has commanded us to pray (Matt 6:5–7; Matt 26:41). So, just like evangelizing, if we do not pray, it shows that we do not belong to God. This is because prayer is conversation with God; it is for primarily God's glory, but also for our benefit.

On the flip side, the very same questions could be asked from the Arminian. If God is not absolutely sovereign, then how can we be sure that God can influence that particular circumstance or event that is directly affecting us? To go further with this question, if the future is open and not entirely determined by God, then how can we be sure that future events after our conversion will lead to our glorification? This is why Calvinism brings great spiritual comfort to the believer. "He who has begun a good work in you will complete it until the day of Jesus Christ" (Phil 1:6). If God chose some for salvation, there is nothing that can thwart God's sovereign will.

— Appendix 2 —

What Does the Bible Say?

It is important to support our theological viewpoints with Scripture. It is important to show that our theology isn't a philosophical invention of man, but God's truth. The Scriptures are the sole highest authority, and thus they have the final say in all truth. If our theology contradicts the Bible, we must revise our theology.

I am firmly convinced that the Bible supports Calvinism. As such, in this appendix I have listed over 250 scriptural references that support the Calvinist position in several theological issues, related to the Calvinism-Arminian debate.

Whose Choice Saves Man?

"Now when the sun was going down, a deep sleep fell upon Abram; and behold, horror and great darkness fell upon him. . . . And it came to pass, when the sun went down and it was dark, that behold, there appeared a smoking oven and a burning torch that passed between those pieces." (Gen 15:12, 17)

"Then He said, 'I will make all My goodness pass before you, and I will proclaim the name of the Lord before you. I will be gracious to whom I will be gracious, and I will have compassion on whom I will have compassion.'" (Exod 33:19)

What Does the Bible Say?

"'You will not need to fight in this battle. Position yourselves, stand still and see the salvation of the Lord, who is with you, O Judah and Jerusalem!' Do not fear or be dismayed; tomorrow go out against them, for the Lord is with you." (2 Chr 20:17)

"Your people shall be volunteers in the day of Your power." (Ps 110:3)

"Then we will not turn back from You; revive us, and we will call upon Your name." (Ps 80:18)

"For there is not a just man on earth who does good and does not sin." (Eccl 7:20)

"Draw me away! We will run after you." (Song 1:4)

"For Jacob My servant's sake, And Israel My elect, I have even called you by your name; I have named you, though you have not known Me." (Isa 45:4)

"Woe to him who strives with his Maker! Let the potsherd strive with the potsherds of the earth! Shall the clay say to him who forms it, 'What are you making?' Or shall your handiwork say, 'He has no hands'?" (Isa 45:9)

"I was sought by those who did not ask for Me; I was found by those who did not seek Me." (Isa 65:1)

"Then I went down to the potter's house, and there he was, making something at the wheel. And the vessel that he made of clay was marred in the hand of the potter; so he made it again into another vessel, as it seemed good to the potter to make. Then the word of the Lord came to me, saying: 'O house of Israel, can I not do with you as this potter?' says the Lord. 'Look, as the clay is in the potter's hand, so are you in My hand, O house of Israel!'" (Jer 18:3–6)

"I have surely heard Ephraim bemoaning himself: 'You have chastised me, and I was chastised, like an untrained bull; restore me, and I will return, for You are the Lord my God.'" (Jer 31:18)

"'I have loved you,' says the Lord. 'Yet you say, "In what way have You loved us?" Was not Esau Jacob's brother?' Says the Lord. 'Yet Jacob I have loved; But Esau I have hated, and laid waste his mountains and his heritage for the jackals of the wilderness.'" (Mal 1:2–3)

Appendix 2

"Or what woman, having ten silver coins, if she loses one coin, does not light a lamp, sweep the house, and search carefully until she finds it? And when she has found it, she calls her friends and neighbors together, saying, 'Rejoice with me, for I have found the piece which I lost!'" (Luke 15:8–9)

"The wind blows where it wishes, and you hear the sound of it, but cannot tell where it comes from and where it goes. So is everyone who is born of the Spirit." (John 3:8)

"John answered and said, 'A man can receive nothing unless it has been given to him from heaven.'" (John 3:27)

"No one can come to Me unless the Father who sent Me draws him; and I will raise him up at the last day." (John 6:44)

"But there are some of you who do not believe. For Jesus knew from the beginning who they were who did not believe, and who would betray Him. And He said, 'Therefore I have said to you that no one can come to Me unless it has been granted to him by My Father.'" (John 6:64–65)

"Therefore if the Son makes you free, you shall be free indeed." (John 8:36)

"You are of your father the devil, and the desires of your father you want to do. He was a murderer from the beginning, and does not stand in the truth, because there is no truth in him. When he speaks a lie, he speaks from his own resources, for he is a liar and the father of it." (John 8:44)

"I am the vine, you are the branches. He who abides in Me, and I in him, bears much fruit; for without Me you can do nothing." (John 15:5)

"You did not choose Me, but I chose you and appointed you that you should go and bear fruit, and that your fruit should remain, that whatever you ask the Father in My name He may give you." (John 15:16)

"If you were of the world, the world would love its own. Yet because you are not of the world, but I chose you out of the world, therefore the world hates you." (John 15:19)

"Repent therefore of this your wickedness, and pray God if perhaps the thought of your heart may be forgiven you." (Acts 8:22)

What Does the Bible Say?

"When they heard these things they became silent; and they glorified God, saying, 'Then God has also granted to the Gentiles repentance to life.'" (Acts 11:18)

"As it is written: 'There is none righteous, no, not one; there is none who understands; here is none who seeks after God. They have all turned aside; they have together become unprofitable; there is none who does good, no, not one.'" (Rom 3:10–12)

"For He says to Moses, 'I will have mercy on whomever I will have mercy, and I will have compassion on whomever I will have compassion.' So then it is not of him who wills, nor of him who runs, but of God who shows mercy." (Rom 9:15–16)

"You will say to me then, 'Why does He still find fault? For who has resisted His will?'" (Rom 9:19)

"Does not the potter have power over the clay, from the same lump to make one vessel for honor and another for dishonor?" (Rom 9:21)

"And that He might make known the riches of His glory on the vessels of mercy, which He had prepared beforehand for glory." (Rom 9:23)

"But Isa is very bold and says, 'I was found by those who did not seek Me; I was made manifest to those who did not ask for Me.'" (Rom 10:20)

"For I say, through the grace given to me, to everyone who is among you, not to think of himself more highly than he ought to think, but to think soberly, as God has dealt to each one a measure of faith." (Rom 12:3)

"I planted, Apollos watered, but God gave the increase. So then neither he who plants is anything, nor he who waters, but God who gives the increase." (1 Cor 3:6–7)

"For who makes you differ from another? And what do you have that you did not receive? Now if you did indeed receive it, why do you boast as if you had not received it?" (1 Cor 4:7)

"For you were bought at a price; therefore glorify God in your body and in your spirit, which are God's." (1 Cor 6:20)

Appendix 2

"Casting down arguments and every high thing that exalts itself against the knowledge of God, bringing every thought into captivity to the obedience of Christ." (2 Cor 10:5)

"But we are bound to give thanks to God always for you, brethren beloved by the Lord, because God from the beginning chose you for salvation through sanctification by the Spirit and belief in the truth." (2 Thess 2:13)

"For by grace you have been saved through faith, and that not of yourselves; it is the gift of God, not of works, lest anyone should boast." (Eph 2:8–9)

"Being confident of this very thing, that He who has begun a good work in you will complete it until the day of Jesus Christ." (Phil 1:6)

"Therefore, my beloved, as you have always obeyed, not as in my presence only, but now much more in my absence, work out your own salvation with fear and trembling; for it is God who works in you both to will and to do for His good pleasure." (Phil 2:12–13)

"But when it pleased God, who separated me from my mother's womb and called me through His grace." (Gal 1:15)

"Therefore do not be ashamed of the testimony of our Lord, nor of me His prisoner, but share with me in the sufferings for the gospel according to the power of God, who has saved us and called us with a holy calling, not according to our works, but according to His own purpose and grace which was given to us in Christ Jesus before time began." (2 Tim 1:8–9)

"The Lord grant to him that he may find mercy from the Lord in that Day—and you know very well how many ways he ministered to me at Ephesus." (2 Tim 1:18)

"And a servant of the Lord must not quarrel but be gentle to all, able to teach, patient, in humility correcting those who are in opposition, if God perhaps will grant them repentance, so that they may know the truth, and that they may come to their senses and escape the snare of the devil, having been taken captive by him to do his will." (2 Tim 2:24–26)

"Therefore, brethren, be even more diligent to make your call and election sure, for if you do these things you will never stumble." (2 Pet 1:10)

"Of His own will He brought us forth by the word of truth, that we might be a kind of firstfruits of His creatures." (Jas 1:18)

"And we know that the Son of God has come and has given us an understanding, that we may know Him who is true; and we are in Him who is true, in His Son Jesus Christ. This is the true God and eternal life." (1 John 5:20)

Concurrence

"The steps of a good man are ordered by the Lord, and He delights in his way." (Ps 37:23)

"You drove out the nations with Your hand, But them You planted; You afflicted the peoples, and cast them out. For they did not gain possession of the land by their own sword, Nor did their own arm save them; But it was Your right hand, Your arm, and the light of Your countenance, Because You favored them." (Ps 44:2–3)

"Teach me Your way, O Lord; I will walk in Your truth; Unite my heart to fear Your name." (Ps 86:11)

"Direct my steps by Your word, And let no iniquity have dominion over me." (Ps 119:133)

"The preparations of the heart belong to man, but the answer of the tongue is from the Lord." (Prov 16:1)

"The king's heart is in the hand of the Lord, Like the rivers of water; He turns it wherever He wishes." (Prov 21:1)

"In those days the Lord began to cut off parts of Israel; and Hazael conquered them in all the territory of Israel." (2 Kgs 10:32)

"All that the Father gives Me will come to Me, and the one who comes to Me I will by no means cast out." (John 6:37)

"And for this reason God will send them strong delusion, that they should believe the lie, that they all may be condemned who did not believe the truth but had pleasure in unrighteousness." (2 Thess 2:6–7)

"Therefore, my beloved, as you have always obeyed, not as in my presence only, but now much more in my absence, work out your own salvation with fear and trembling; for it is God who works in you both to will and to do for His good pleasure." (Phil 2:12–13)

"But in a great house there are not only vessels of gold and silver, but also of wood and clay, some for honor and some for dishonor. Therefore if anyone cleanses himself from the latter, he will be a vessel for honor, sanctified and useful for the Master, prepared for every good work." (2 Tim 2:20–21)

Does God Elect Some People?

"Yet I have reserved seven thousand in Israel, all whose knees have not bowed to Baal, and every mouth that has not kissed him." (1 Kgs 19:18)

"He answered and said to them, 'Because it has been given to you to know the mysteries of the kingdom of heaven, but to them it has not been given.'" (Matt 13:11)

"But when the first came, they supposed that they would receive more; and they likewise received each a denarius. And when they had received it, they complained against the landowner, saying, 'These last men have worked only one hour, and you made them equal to us who have borne the burden and the heat of the day.' But he answered one of them and said, 'Friend, I am doing you no wrong. Did you not agree with me for a denarius? Take what is yours and go your way. I wish to give to this last man the same as to you. Is it not lawful for me to do what I wish with my own things? Or is your eye evil because I am good?' So the last will be first, and the first last. For many are called, but few chosen." (Matt 20:10–16)

"Nevertheless do not rejoice in this, that the spirits are subject to you, but rather rejoice because your names are written in heaven." (Luke 10:20)

"And some of the Pharisees called to Him from the crowd, 'Teacher, rebuke Your disciples.' But He answered and said to them, 'I tell you that if these should keep silent, the stones would immediately cry out.'" (Luke 19:39–40)

"For as the Father raises the dead and gives life to them, even so the Son gives life to whom He will." (John 5:21)

"He who is of God hears God's words; therefore you do not hear, because you are not of God." (John 8:47)

"My Father, who has given them to Me, is greater than all; and no one is able to snatch them out of My Father's hand." (John 10:29)

"As You have given Him authority over all flesh, that He should give eternal life to as many as You have given Him." (John 17:2)

"I have manifested Your name to the men whom You have given Me out of the world. They were Yours, You gave them to Me, and they have kept Your word." (John 17:6)

"For many walk, of whom I have told you often, and now tell you even weeping, that they are the enemies of the cross of Christ: whose end is destruction, whose god is their belly, and whose glory is in their shame—who set their mind on earthly things." (Phil 3:19–20)

"Knowing, beloved brethren, your election by God." (1 Thess 1:4)

"Therefore, in all things He had to be made like His brethren, that He might be a merciful and faithful High Priest in things pertaining to God, to make propitiation for the sins of the people." (Heb 2:17)

"And I saw the dead, small and great, standing before God, and books were opened. And another book was opened, which is the Book of Life. And the dead were judged according to their works, by the things which were written in the books." (Rev 20:12)

Whom Does God Call to Salvation?

"And if you are willing to receive it, he is Elijah who is to come. He who has ears to hear, let him hear!" (Matt 11:14–15)

"'He who has ears to hear, let him hear!' And the disciples came and said to Him, 'Why do You speak to them in parables?' He answered and said to them, 'Because it has been given to you to know the mysteries of the kingdom of heaven, but to them it has not been given.'" (Matt 13:9–11)

"But He said to them, 'All cannot accept this saying, but only those to whom it has been given.'" (Matt 19:11)

Appendix 2

"But when the king came in to see the guests, he saw a man there who did not have on a wedding garment. So he said to him, 'Friend, how did you come in here without a wedding garment?' And he was speechless. Then the king said to the servants, 'Bind him hand and foot, take him away, and cast him into outer darkness; there will be weeping and gnashing of teeth.' For many are called, but few are chosen." (Matt 22:11–14)

"And He said to them, 'He who has ears to hear, let him hear!' But when He was alone, those around Him with the twelve asked Him about the parable. And He said to them, 'To you it has been given to know the mystery of the kingdom of God; but to those who are outside, all things come in parables.'" (Mark 4:9–11)

"If anyone has ears to hear, let him hear." (Mark 4:23)

"When He had said these things He cried, 'He who has ears to hear, let him hear!' Then His disciples asked Him, saying, 'What does this parable mean?' And He said, 'To you it has been given to know the mysteries of the kingdom of God, but to the rest it is given in parables, that 'Seeing they may not see, and hearing they may not understand.'" (Luke 8:8–10)

"It is neither fit for the land nor for the dunghill, but men throw it out. He who has ears to hear, let him hear!" (Luke 14:35)

"He who has an ear, let him hear what the Spirit says to the churches. To him who overcomes I will give to eat from the tree of life, which is in the midst of the Paradise of God." (Rev 2:7)

"He who has an ear, let him hear what the Spirit says to the churches." (Rev 3:13, 22)

"'Let us be glad and rejoice and give Him glory, for the marriage of the Lamb has come, and His wife has made herself ready.' And to her it was granted to be arrayed in fine linen, clean and bright, for the fine linen is the righteous acts of the saints." (Rev 19:7–8)

God Determines All Things

"The counsel of the Lord stands forever, the plans of His heart to all generations." (Ps 33:11)

"Whatever the Lord pleases He does, in heaven and in earth, in the seas and in all deep places." (Ps 135:6)

"The lot is cast into the lap, but its every decision is from the Lord." (Prov 16:33)

"Remember the former things of old, For I am God, and there is no other; I am God, and there is none like Me, Declaring the end from the beginning, and from ancient times things that are not yet done, Saying, 'My counsel shall stand, And I will do all My pleasure,' Calling a bird of prey from the east, The man who executes My counsel, from a far country. Indeed I have spoken it; I will also bring it to pass. I have purposed it; I will also do it." (Isa 46:9–11)

"'For this is like the waters of Noah to Me; for as I have sworn that the waters of Noah would no longer cover the earth, so have I sworn that I would not be angry with you, nor rebuke you. For the mountains shall depart and the hills be removed, but My kindness shall not depart from you nor shall My covenant of peace be removed,' says the Lord, who has mercy on you." (Isa 54:9–10)

"It shall come to pass that before they call, I will answer; and while they are still speaking, I will hear." (Isa 65:24)

"In Him also we have obtained an inheritance, being predestined according to the purpose of Him who works all things according to the counsel of His will." (Eph 1:11)

"For in Him we live and move and have our being, as also some of your own poets have said, 'For we are also His offspring.'" (Acts 17:28)

Man's Inability

"And I will harden Pharaoh's heart, and multiply My signs and My wonders in the land of Egypt." (Exod 7:3)

"And Pharaoh's heart grew hard, and he did not heed them, as the Lord had said." (Exod 7:13)

"But when Pharaoh saw that there was relief, he hardened his heart and did not heed them, as the Lord had said." (Exod 8:15)

Appendix 2

"But Pharaoh hardened his heart at this time also; neither would he let the people go." (Exod 8:32)

"But the Lord hardened the heart of Pharaoh; and he did not heed them, just as the Lord had spoken to Moses." (Exod 9:12)

"Now the Lord said to Moses, 'Go in to Pharaoh; for I have hardened his heart and the hearts of his servants, that I may show these signs of Mine before him.'" (Exod 10:1)

"But the Lord hardened Pharaoh's heart, and he did not let the children of Israel go." (Exod 10:20)

"But the Lord hardened Pharaoh's heart, and he would not let them go." (Exod 10:27)

"So Moses and Aaron did all these wonders before Pharaoh; and the Lord hardened Pharaoh's heart, and he did not let the children of Israel go out of his land." (Exod 11:10)

"'Then I will harden Pharaoh's heart, so that he will pursue them; and I will gain honor over Pharaoh and over all his army, that the Egyptians may know that I am the Lord.' And they did so. . .And the Lord hardened the heart of Pharaoh king of Egypt, and he pursued the children of Israel; and the children of Israel went out with boldness." (Exod 14:4, 8)

"I will give you a new heart and put a new spirit within you; I will take the heart of stone out of your flesh and give you a heart of flesh." (Ezek 36:26)

"But as many as received Him, to them He gave the right to become children of God, to those who believe in His name: who were born, not of blood, nor of the will of the flesh, nor of the will of man, but of God." (John 1:12–13)

"And I will pray the Father, and He will give you another Helper, that He may abide with you forever—the Spirit of truth, whom the world cannot receive, because it neither sees Him nor knows Him; but you know Him, for He dwells with you and will be in you." (John 14:16–17)

"For to be carnally minded is death, but to be spiritually minded is life and peace. Because the carnal mind is enmity against God; for it is not subject to the law of God, nor indeed can be. So then, those who are in the flesh cannot please God." (Rom 8:6–8)

"Among whom also we all once conducted ourselves in the lusts of our flesh, fulfilling the desires of the flesh and of the mind, and were by nature children of wrath, just as the others." (Eph 2:3)

"But the natural man does not receive the things of the Spirit of God, for they are foolishness to him; nor can he know them, because they are spiritually discerned." (1 Cor 2:14)

"But even if our gospel is veiled, it is veiled to those who are perishing, whose minds the god of this age has blinded, who do not believe, lest the light of the gospel of the glory of Christ, who is the image of God, should shine on them." (2 Cor 4:3–4)

"But the fruit of the Spirit is love, joy, peace, longsuffering, kindness, goodness, faithfulness, gentleness, self-control. Against such there is no law." (Gal 5:22–23)

Our Nature Defines Us, Not Our Will

"God is not a man, that He should lie, nor a son of man, that He should repent." (Num 23:19)

"Who can bring a clean thing out of an unclean? No one!" (Job 14:4)

"The wicked are estranged from the womb; They go astray as soon as they are born, speaking lies." (Ps 58:3)

"You are of your father the devil, and the desires of your father you want to do. He was a murderer from the beginning, and does not stand in the truth, because there is no truth in him. When he speaks a lie, he speaks from his own resources, for he is a liar and the father of it." (John 8:44)

"Among whom also we all once conducted ourselves in the lusts of our flesh, fulfilling the desires of the flesh and of the mind, and were by nature children of wrath, just as the others." (Eph 2:3)

"In hope of eternal life which God, who cannot lie, promised before time began." (Titus 1:2)

Appendix 2

Who Did Jesus Die For?

"He was taken from prison and from judgment, and who will declare His generation? For He was cut off from the land of the living; for the transgressions of My people He was stricken." (Isa 53:8)

"He shall see the labor of His soul, and be satisfied. By His knowledge My righteous Servant shall justify many, for He shall bear their iniquities. Therefore I will divide Him a portion with the great, and He shall divide the spoil with the strong, because He poured out His soul unto death, and He was numbered with the transgressors, and He bore the sin of many, and made intercession for the transgressors." (Isa 53:11–12)

"And she will bring forth a Son, and you shall call His name Jesus, for He will save His people from their sins." (Matt 1:21)

"Just as the Son of Man did not come to be served, but to serve, and to give His life a ransom for many." (Matt 20:28)

"For this is My blood of the new covenant, which is shed for many for the remission of sins." (Matt 26:28)

"For even the Son of Man did not come to be served, but to serve, and to give His life a ransom for many." (Mark 10:45)

"And He said to them, 'This is My blood of the new covenant, which is shed for many.'" (Mark 14:24)

"I am the good shepherd. The good shepherd gives His life for the sheep." (John 10:11)

"Greater love has no one than this, than to lay down one's life for his friends." (John 15:13)

"I pray for them. I do not pray for the world but for those whom You have given Me, for they are Yours." (John 17:9)

"Father, I desire that they also whom You gave Me may be with Me where I am, that they may behold My glory which You have given Me; for You loved Me before the foundation of the world." (John 17:24)

"Jesus answered, 'I have told you that I am He. Therefore, if you seek Me, let these go their way,' that the saying might be fulfilled which He spoke, 'Of those whom You gave Me I have lost none.'" (John 18:8–9)

"Therefore take heed to yourselves and to all the flock, among which the Holy Spirit has made you overseers, to shepherd the church of God which He purchased with His own blood." (Acts 20:28)

"He who did not spare His own Son, but delivered Him up for us all, how shall He not with Him also freely give us all things?" (Rom 8:32)

"I have been crucified with Christ; it is no longer I who live, but Christ lives in me; and the life which I now live in the flesh I live by faith in the Son of God, who loved me and gave Himself for me." (Gal 2:20)

"Husbands, love your wives, just as Christ also loved the church and gave Himself for her." (Ephesians 5:25)

"For to this end we both labor and suffer reproach, because we trust in the living God, who is the Savior of all men, especially of those who believe." (1 Tim 4:10)

"So Christ was offered once to bear the sins of many." (Heb 9:28)

"By faith Noah, being divinely warned of things not yet seen, moved with godly fear, prepared an ark for the saving of his household, by which he condemned the world and became heir of the righteousness which is according to faith." (Heb 11:7)

"Then a white robe was given to each of them; and it was said to them that they should rest a little while longer, until both the number of their fellow servants and their brethren, who would be killed as they were, was completed." (Rev 6:11)

Does God Foreordain Some to Hell?

"Yet the Lord has not given you a heart to perceive and eyes to see and ears to hear, to this very day." (Deut 29:4)

"For the wicked are reserved for the day of doom; They shall be brought out on the day of wrath." (Job 21:30)

Appendix 2

"You have rebuked the nations, You have destroyed the wicked; You have blotted out their name forever and ever." (Ps 9:5)

"So I gave them over to their own stubborn heart, to walk in their own counsels." (Ps 81:12)

"The Lord has made all for Himself, Yes, even the wicked for the day of doom." (Prov 16:4)

"And He said, 'Go, and tell this people: Keep on hearing, but do not understand; keep on seeing, but do not perceive.' 'Make the heart of this people dull, and their ears heavy, and shut their eyes; lest they see with their eyes, and hear with their ears, and understand with their heart, and return and be healed.'" (Isa 6:9–10)

"He who believes in Him is not condemned; but he who does not believe is condemned already, because he has not believed in the name of the only begotten Son of God." (John 3:18)

"Jesus answered them, 'Did I not choose you, the twelve, and one of you is a devil?'" (John 6:70)

"He who is of God hears God's words; therefore you do not hear, because you are not of God." (John 8:47)

"And Jesus said, 'For judgment I have come into this world, that those who do not see may see, and that those who see may be made blind.'" (John 9:39)

"But you do not believe, because you are not of My sheep, as I said to you." (John 10:26)

"Therefore they could not believe, because Isa said again: 'He has blinded their eyes and hardened their hearts, lest they should see with their eyes, lest they should understand with their hearts and turn, so that I should heal them.'" (John 12:39–40)

"While I was with them in the world, I kept them in Your name. Those whom You gave Me I have kept; and none of them is lost except the son of perdition, that the Scripture might be fulfilled." (John 17:12)

What Does the Bible Say?

"Therefore God also gave them up to uncleanness, in the lusts of their hearts, to dishonor their bodies among themselves, who exchanged the truth of God for the lie, and worshiped and served the creature rather than the Creator, who is blessed forever. Amen. For this reason God gave them up to vile passions. For even their women exchanged the natural use for what is against nature. Likewise also the men, leaving the natural use of the woman, burned in their lust for one another, men with men committing what is shameful, and receiving in themselves the penalty of their error which was due. And even as they did not like to retain God in their knowledge, God gave them over to a debased mind, to do those things which are not fitting." (Rom 1:24–28)

"Does not the potter have power over the clay, from the same lump to make one vessel for honor and another for dishonor?" (Rom 9:21)

"Just as it is written: 'God has given them a spirit of stupor, eyes that they should not see and ears that they should not hear, to this very day.'" (Rom 11:8)

"For we are to God the fragrance of Christ among those who are being saved and among those who are perishing." (2 Cor 2:15)

"He died for all, that those who live should live no longer for themselves, but for Him who died for them and rose again." (2 Cor 5:15)

"Let no one deceive you by any means; for that Day will not come unless the falling away comes first, and the man of sin is revealed, the son of perdition." (2 Thess 2:13)

"But there were also false prophets among the people, even as there will be false teachers among you, who will secretly bring in destructive heresies, even denying the Lord who bought them, and bring on themselves swift destruction. And many will follow their destructive ways, because of whom the way of truth will be blasphemed. By covetousness they will exploit you with deceptive words; for a long time their judgment has not been idle, and their destruction does not slumber." (2 Pet 2:1–3)

"For certain men have crept in unnoticed, who long ago were marked out for this condemnation, ungodly men, who turn the grace of our God into lewdness and deny the only Lord God and our Lord Jesus Christ." (Jude 1:4)

Appendix 2

Does God Hate Some People?

"I will set My face against you, and you shall be defeated by your enemies. Those who hate you shall reign over you, and you shall flee when no one pursues you." (Lev 26:17)

"God is a just judge, And God is angry with the wicked every day." (Ps 7:11)

"The Lord tests the righteous, but the wicked and the one who loves violence His soul hates. Upon the wicked He will rain coals; fire and brimstone and a burning wind shall be the portion of their cup." (Ps 11:5–6)

"The sacrifice of the wicked is an abomination to the Lord, but the prayer of the upright is His delight. The way of the wicked is an abomination to the Lord, but He loves him who follows righteousness." (Prov 5:8–9)

"As it is written, 'Jacob I have loved, but Esau I have hated.'" (Rom 9:13)

"Therefore I was angry with that generation, and said, 'They always go astray in their heart, and they have not known My ways.' So I swore in My wrath, 'They shall not enter My rest.'" (Heb 3:10–11)

Does God Bring Calamity on Certain People?

"Then the Lord saw that the wickedness of man was great in the earth, and that every intent of the thoughts of his heart was only evil continually. And the Lord was sorry that He had made man on the earth, and He was grieved in His heart. So the Lord said, 'I will destroy man whom I have created from the face of the earth, both man and beast, creeping thing and birds of the air, for I am sorry that I have made them.'" (Gen 6:5–7)

"So the Lord said to him, 'Who has made man's mouth? Or who makes the mute, the deaf, the seeing, or the blind? Have not I, the Lord?'" (Exod 4:11)

"And I indeed will harden the hearts of the Egyptians, and they shall follow them. So I will gain honor over Pharaoh and over all his army, his chariots, and his horsemen. Then the Egyptians shall know that I am the Lord, when I have gained honor for Myself over Pharaoh, his chariots, and his horsemen." (Exod 14:17–18)

What Does the Bible Say?

"I will set My face against you, and you shall be defeated by your enemies. Those who hate you shall reign over you, and you shall flee when no one pursues you." (Lev 26:17)

"Who fed you in the wilderness with manna, which your fathers did not know, that He might humble you and that He might test you, to do you good in the end." (Deut 8:16)

"Wherever they went out, the hand of the Lord was against them for calamity, as the Lord had said, and as the Lord had sworn to them. And they were greatly distressed." (Judg 2:15)

"The Lord makes poor and makes rich; He brings low and lifts up." (1 Sam 2:7)

"Then the king said to Zadok, 'Carry the ark of God back into the city. If I find favor in the eyes of the Lord, He will bring me back and show me both it and His dwelling place. But if He says thus: "I have no delight in you," here I am, let Him do to me as seems good to Him.'" (2 Sam 15:25–26)

"Again the anger of the Lord was aroused against Israel, and He moved David against them to say, 'Go, number Israel and Judah.' . . . And David's heart condemned him after he had numbered the people. So David said to the Lord, 'I have sinned greatly in what I have done; but now, I pray, O Lord, take away the iniquity of Your servant, for I have done very foolishly.'" (2 Sam 24:1, 10)

"Then they will answer, 'Because they forsook the Lord their God, who brought their fathers out of the land of Egypt, and have embraced other gods, and worshiped them and served them; therefore the Lord has brought all this calamity on them.'" (1 Kgs 9:9)

"Then he cried out to the Lord and said, 'O Lord my God, have You also brought tragedy on the widow with whom I lodge, by killing her son?'" (1 Kgs 17:20)

"Then he said to him, 'Thus says the Lord: Because you have let slip out of your hand a man whom I appointed to utter destruction, therefore your life shall go for his life, and your people for his people.'" (1 Kgs 20:42)

Appendix 2

"Behold, I will bring calamity on you. I will take away your posterity, and will cut off from Ahab every male in Israel, both bond and free. . . . See how Ahab has humbled himself before Me? Because he has humbled himself before Me, I will not bring the calamity in his days. In the days of his son I will bring the calamity on his house." (1 Kgs 21:21, 29)

"And while he was still talking with them, there was the messenger, coming down to him; and then the king said, 'Surely this calamity is from the Lord; why should I wait for the Lord any longer?'" (2 Kgs 6:33)

"And the Lord said to Jehu, 'Because you have done well in doing what is right in My sight, and have done to the house of Ahab all that was in My heart, your sons shall sit on the throne of Israel to the fourth generation.'" (2 Kgs 10:30)

"In those days the Lord began to cut off parts of Israel; and Hazael conquered them in all the territory of Israel." (2 Kgs 10:32)

"Therefore thus says the Lord God of Israel: 'Behold, I am bringing such calamity upon Jerusalem and Judah, that whoever hears of it, both his ears will tingle.'" (2 Kgs 21:12)

"Thus says the Lord: 'Behold, I will bring calamity on this place and on its inhabitants—all the words of the book which the king of Judah has read.'" (2 Kgs 22:16)

"And the Lord sent against him raiding bands of Chaldeans, bands of Syrians, bands of Moabites, and bands of the people of Ammon; He sent them against Judah to destroy it, according to the word of the Lord which He had spoken by His servants the prophets. Surely at the commandment of the Lord this came upon Judah, to remove them from His sight because of the sins of Manasseh, according to all that he had done." (2 Kgs 24:2–3)

"So nation was destroyed by nation, and city by city, for God troubled them with every adversity." (2 Chr 15:6)

"Moreover the Lord stirred up against Jehoram the spirit of the Philistines and the Arabians who were near the Ethiopians." (2 Chr 21:16)

"His going to Joram was God's occasion for Ahaziah's downfall; for when he arrived, he went out with Jehoram against Jehu the son of Nimshi, whom the Lord had anointed to cut off the house of Ahab." (2 Chr 22:7)

"Naked I came from my mother's womb, and naked shall I return there. The Lord gave, and the Lord has taken away; blessed be the name of the Lord." (Job 1:21)

"But he said to her, 'You speak as one of the foolish women speaks. Shall we indeed accept good from God, and shall we not accept adversity?' In all this Job did not sin with his lips." (Job 2:10)

"He shall cut off the spirit of princes; He is awesome to the Kgs of the earth." (Ps 76:12)

"I also will laugh at your calamity; I will mock when your terror comes." (Prov 1:26)

"For My sword shall be bathed in heaven; indeed it shall come down on Edom, and on the people of My curse, for judgment." (Isa 34:5)

"I form the light and create darkness, I make peace and create calamity; I, the Lord, do all these things." (Isa 45:7)

"For the iniquity of his covetousness I was angry and struck him; I hid and was angry, and he went on backsliding in the way of his heart." (Isa 57:17)

"Yet it pleased the Lord to bruise Him; He has put Him to grief. When You make His soul an offering for sin"; "Saying, 'I have sinned by betraying innocent blood.' And they said, 'What is that to us? You see to it!'" (Isa 53:10; Matt 27:4)

"If that nation against whom I have spoken turns from its evil, I will relent of the disaster that I thought to bring upon it." (Jer 18:8)

"Now therefore, speak to the men of Judah and to the inhabitants of Jerusalem, saying, 'Thus says the Lord: "Behold, I am fashioning a disaster and devising a plan against you. Return now every one from his evil way, and make your ways and your doings good."'" (Jer 18:11)

"Is it not from the mouth of the Most High that woe and well-being proceed?" (Lam 3:38)

"You only have I known of all the families of the earth; therefore I will punish you for all your iniquities." (Amos 3:2)

Appendix 2

"Are not two sparrows sold for a copper coin? And not one of them falls to the ground apart from your Father's will." (Matt 10:29)

"He went a little farther and fell on His face, and prayed, saying, 'O My Father, if it is possible, let this cup pass from Me; nevertheless, not as I will, but as You will.'" (Matt 26:39)

"Jesus answered, "You could have no power at all against Me unless it had been given you from above. Therefore the one who delivered Me to you has the greater sin.'" (John 19:11)

"Then Paul answered, 'What do you mean by weeping and breaking my heart? For I am ready not only to be bound, but also to die at Jerusalem for the name of the Lord Jesus.' So when he would not be persuaded, we ceased, saying, 'The will of the Lord be done.'" (Acts 21:13–14)

"Since it is a righteous thing with God to repay with tribulation those who trouble you, and to give you who are troubled rest with us when the Lord Jesus is revealed from heaven with His mighty angels, in flaming fire taking vengeance on those who do not know God, and on those who do not obey the gospel of our Lord Jesus Christ. These shall be punished with everlasting destruction from the presence of the Lord and from the glory of His power." (2 Thess 1:6–9)

"And for this reason God will send them strong delusion, that they should believe the lie." (2 Thess 2:11)

"Another horse, fiery red, went out. And it was granted to the one who sat on it to take peace from the earth, and that people should kill one another; and there was given to him a great sword." (Rev 6:4)

"These are the two olive trees and the two lampstands standing before the God of the earth. And if anyone wants to harm them, fire proceeds from their mouth and devours their enemies. And if anyone wants to harm them, he must be killed in this manner. These have power to shut heaven, so that no rain falls in the days of their prophecy; and they have power over waters to turn them to blood, and to strike the earth with all plagues, as often as they desire. When they finish their testimony, the beast that ascends out of the bottomless pit will make war against them, overcome them, and kill them." (Rev 11:4–7)

"It was granted to him to make war with the saints and to overcome them. And authority was given him over every tribe, tongue, and nation." (Rev 13:7)

"Render to her just as she rendered to you, and repay her double according to her works; in the cup which she has mixed, mix double for her." (Rev 18:6)

Does All Always Mean Every Single Thing or Person?

"I will bless those who bless you, And I will curse him who curses you; And in you all the families of the earth shall be blessed." (Gen 12:3)

"Then the Lord spoke to Moses, 'Say to Aaron, Take your rod and stretch out your hand over the waters of Egypt, over their streams, over their rivers, over their ponds, and over all their pools of water, that they may become blood. And there shall be blood throughout all the land of Egypt, both in buckets of wood and pitchers of stone.'" (Exod 7:19)

"Now all the people were in a dispute throughout all the tribes of Israel, saying, 'The king saved us from the hand of our enemies, he delivered us from the hand of the Philistines, and now he has fled from the land because of Absalom.'" (2 Sam 19:9)

"Then King Rehoboam sent Adoram, who was in charge of the revenue; but all Israel stoned him with stones, and he died. Therefore King Rehoboam mounted his chariot in haste to flee to Jerusalem." (1 Kgs 12:18)

"And when Rehoboam came to Jerusalem, he assembled all the house of Judah with the tribe of Benjamin, one hundred and eighty thousand chosen men who were warriors, to fight against the house of Israel, that he might restore the kingdom to Rehoboam the son of Solomon." (1 Kgs 12:21)

"Now therefore, send and gather all Israel to me on Mount Carmel, the four hundred and fifty prophets of Baal, and the four hundred prophets of Asherah, who eat at Jezebel's table." (1 Kgs 18:19)

Appendix 2

"When Athaliah the mother of Ahaziah saw that her son was dead, she arose and destroyed all the royal heirs. But Jehosheba, the daughter of King Joram, sister of Ahaziah, took Joash the son of Ahaziah, and stole him away from among the king's sons who were being murdered; and they hid him and his nurse in the bedroom, from Athaliah, so that he was not killed." (2 Kgs 11:1–2)

"And all the people of the land went to the temple of Baal, and tore it down. They thoroughly broke in pieces its altars and images, and killed Mattan the priest of Baal before the altars. And the priest appointed officers over the house of the Lord." (2 Kgs 11:18)

"Then Jehoshaphat stood in the assembly of Judah and Jerusalem, in the house of the Lord, before the new court. . . . Now all Judah, with their little ones, their wives, and their children, stood before the Lord." (2 Chr 20:5, 13)

"Now when Athaliah the mother of Ahaziah saw that her son was dead, she arose and destroyed all the royal heirs of the house of Judah. But Jehoshabeath, the daughter of the king, took Joash the son of Ahaziah, and stole him away from among the king's sons who were being murdered, and put him and his nurse in a bedroom. So Jehoshabeath, the daughter of King Jehoram, the wife of Jehoiada the priest (for she was the sister of Ahaziah), hid him from Athaliah so that she did not kill him." (2 Chr 22:10–11)

"Thus says Cyrus king of Persia: All the kingdoms of the earth the Lord God of heaven has given me." (Ezra 1:2)

"He is driven from light into darkness, and chased out of the world." (Job 18:18)

"He shall judge the world in righteousness, and He shall administer judgment for the peoples in uprightness." (Ps 9:8)

"All the ends of the world Shall remember and turn to the Lord, and all the families of the nations Shall worship before You." (Ps 22:27)

"For He is coming, for He is coming to judge the earth. He shall judge the world with righteousness, and the peoples with His truth." (Ps 96:13)

"I will punish the world for its evil, And the wicked for their iniquity; I will halt the arrogance of the proud, and will lay low the haughtiness of the terrible." (Isa 13:11)

What Does the Bible Say?

"With my soul I have desired You in the night, Yes, by my spirit within me I will seek You early; For when Your judgments are in the earth, The inhabitants of the world will learn righteousness." (Isa 26:9)

"Then Jerusalem, all Judea, and all the region around the Jordan went out to him." (Matt 3:5)

"Then all the land of Judea, and those from Jerusalem, went out to him and were all baptized by him in the Jordan River, confessing their sins." (Mark 1:5)

"And it came to pass in those days that a decree went out from Caesar Augustus that all the world should be registered." (Luke 2:1)

"And they will fall by the edge of the sword, and be led away captive into all nations. And Jerusalem will be trampled by Gentiles until the times of the Gentiles are fulfilled." (Luke 21:24)

"And many of the Samaritans of that city believed in Him because of the word of the woman who testified, 'He told me all that I ever did.'" (John 4:39)

"The world cannot hate you, but it hates Me because I testify of it that its works are evil." (John 7:7)

"The Pharisees therefore said among themselves, 'You see that you are accomplishing nothing. Look, the world has gone after Him!'" (John 12:19)

"And I, if I am lifted up from the earth, will draw all peoples to Myself." (John 12:32)

"And if anyone hears My words and does not believe, I do not judge him; for I did not come to judge the world but to save the world." (John 12:47)

"Judas (not Iscariot) said to Him, 'Lord, how is it that You will manifest Yourself to us, and not to the world?'" (John 14:22)

"If the world hates you, you know that it hated Me before it hated you. If you were of the world, the world would love its own. Yet because you are not of the world, but I chose you out of the world, therefore the world hates you." (John 15:18–19)

Appendix 2

"I have given them Your word; and the world has hated them because they are not of the world, just as I am not of the world." (John 17:14)

"After this, Jesus, knowing that all things were now accomplished, that the Scripture might be fulfilled, said, 'I thirst!'" (John 19:28)

"And it shall come to pass in the last days, says God, that I will pour out of My Spirit on all flesh." (Acts 2:17a)

"Nor is He worshiped with men's hands, as though He needed anything, since He gives to all life, breath, and all things." (Acts 17:25)

"So not only is this trade of ours in danger of falling into disrepute, but also the temple of the great goddess Diana may be despised and her magnificence destroyed, whom all Asia and the world worship." (Acts 19:27)

"First, I thank my God through Jesus Christ for you all, that your faith is spoken of throughout the whole world." (Rom 1:8)

"He who did not spare His own Son, but delivered Him up for us all, how shall He not with Him also freely give us all things?" (Rom 8:32)

"But it is not that the word of God has taken no effect. For they are not all Israel who are of Israel." (Rom 9:6)

"For if their being cast away is the reconciling of the world, what will their acceptance be but life from the dead?" (Rom 11:15)

"Do you not know that the saints will judge the world? And if the world will be judged by you, are you unworthy to judge the smallest matters?" (1 Cor 6:2)

"All things are lawful for me, but all things are not helpful. All things are lawful for me, but I will not be brought under the power of any." (1 Cor 6:12)

"And there are diversities of activities, but it is the same God who works all in all." (1 Cor 12:6)

"That is, that God was in Christ reconciling the world to Himself, not imputing their trespasses to them, and has committed to us the word of reconciliation." (2 Cor 5:19)

What Does the Bible Say?

"But that you also may know my affairs and how I am doing, Tychicus, a beloved brother and faithful minister in the Lord, will make all things known to you." (Eph 6:21)

"Therefore I exhort first of all that supplications, prayers, intercessions, and giving of thanks be made for all men, for kings and all who are in authority, that we may lead a quiet and peaceable life in all godliness and reverence." (1 Tim 2:1–2)

"For who, having heard, rebelled? Indeed, was it not all who came out of Egypt, led by Moses? Now with whom was He angry forty years? Was it not with those who sinned, whose corpses fell in the wilderness? And to whom did He swear that they would not enter His rest, but to those who did not obey?" (Heb 3:16–18)

"Behold what manner of love the Father has bestowed on us, that we should be called children of God! Therefore the world does not know us, because it did not know Him." (1 John 3:1)

"Do not marvel, my brethren, if the world hates you." (1 John 3:13)

"You are of God, little children, and have overcome them, because He who is in you is greater than he who is in the world. They are of the world. Therefore they speak as of the world, and the world hears them."(1 John 4:4–5)

"We know that we are of God, and the whole world lies under the sway of the wicked one." (1 John 5:19)

"Because you have kept My command to persevere, I also will keep you from the hour of trial which shall come upon the whole world, to test those who dwell on the earth." (Rev 3:10)

"So the great dragon was cast out, that serpent of old, called the Devil and Satan, who deceives the whole world; he was cast to the earth, and his angels were cast out with him." (Rev 12:9)

"And I saw one of his heads as if it had been mortally wounded, and his deadly wound was healed. And all the world marveled and followed the beast." (Rev 13:3)

Appendix 2

"For they are spirits of demons, performing signs, which go out to the kings of the earth and of the whole world, to gather them to the battle of that great day of God Almighty." (Rev 16:14)

"And the nations of those who are saved shall walk in its light, and the kings of the earth bring their glory and honor into it." (Rev 21:24)

Total Depravity

"Then the Lord saw that the wickedness of man was great in the earth, and that every intent of the thoughts of his heart was only evil continually." (Gen 6:5)

"And the king of Israel said to Jehoshaphat, 'I will disguise myself and go into battle; but you put on your robes.' So the king of Israel disguised himself and went into battle. Now the king of Syria had commanded the thirty-two captains of his chariots, saying, 'Fight with no one small or great, but only with the king of Israel.' So it was, when the captains of the chariots saw Jehoshaphat, that they said, 'Surely it is the king of Israel!' Therefore they turned aside to fight against him, and Jehoshaphat cried out. And it happened, when the captains of the chariots saw that it was not the king of Israel, that they turned back from pursuing him." (1 Kgs 22:30–33)

"Who can bring a clean thing out of an unclean? No one!" (Job 14:4)

"All day they twist my words; all their thoughts are against me for evil." (Ps 56:5)

"Son of man, these bones are the whole house of Israel. They indeed say, 'Our bones are dry, our hope is lost, and we ourselves are cut off!'" (Ezek 37:11)

"He was in the world, and the world was made through Him, and the world did not know Him. He came to His own, and His own did not receive Him." (John 1:10–11)

"If the world hates you, you know that it hated Me before it hated you." (John 15:18)

"As it is written: 'There is none righteous, no, not one; there is none who understands; here is none who seeks after God. They have all turned aside; they have together become unprofitable; there is none who does good, no, not one.'" (Rom 3:10–12)

"For when you were slaves of sin, you were free in regard to righteousness." (Rom 6:20)

"But the natural man does not receive the things of the Spirit of God, for they are foolishness to him; nor can he know them, because they are spiritually discerned." (1 Cor 2:14)

"Whose minds the god of this age has blinded, who do not believe, lest the light of the gospel of the glory of Christ, who is the image of God, should shine on them." (2 Cor 4:4)

"And you, being dead in your trespasses and the uncircumcision of your flesh, He has made alive together with Him, having forgiven you all trespasses." (Col 2:13)

"These are the two olive trees and the two lampstands standing before the God of the earth. And if anyone wants to harm them, fire proceeds from their mouth and devours their enemies. And if anyone wants to harm them, he must be killed in this manner. These have power to shut heaven, so that no rain falls in the days of their prophecy; and they have power over waters to turn them to blood, and to strike the earth with all plagues, as often as they desire." (Rev 11:4–6)

"And all the world marveled and followed the beast." (Rev 13:3)

The "Ordo Salutis" (Election, Call, Regeneration, Faith, Justification, Adoption, Sanctification, Perseverance, Glorification)

"Do not marvel that I said to you, 'You must be born again.' The wind blows where it wishes, and you hear the sound of it, but cannot tell where it comes from and where it goes. So is everyone who is born of the Spirit." (John 3:7–8)

"All that the Father gives Me will come to Me, and the one who comes to Me I will by no means cast out." (John 6:37)

Appendix 2

"No one can come to Me unless the Father who sent Me draws him; and I will raise him up at the last day." (John 6:44)

"To demonstrate at the present time His righteousness, that He might be just and the justifier of the one who has faith in Jesus. . . .Therefore we conclude that a man is justified by faith apart from the deeds of the law. . . . Since there is one God who will justify the circumcised by faith and the uncircumcised through faith." (Rom 3:26, 28, 30)

"For whom He foreknew, He also predestined to be conformed to the image of His Son, that He might be the firstborn among many brethren. Moreover whom He predestined, these He also called; whom He called, these He also justified; and whom He justified, these He also glorified." (Rom 8:29–30)

"And that He might make known the riches of His glory on the vessels of mercy, which He had prepared beforehand for glory." (Rom 9:23)

"Now when the Gentiles heard this, they were glad and glorified the word of the Lord. And as many as had been appointed to eternal life believed." (Acts 13:48)

"Just as He chose us in Him before the foundation of the world, that we should be holy and without blame before Him in love, having predestined us to adoption as sons by Jesus Christ to Himself, according to the good pleasure of His will." (Eph 1:4–5)

"But we are bound to give thanks to God always for you, brethren beloved by the Lord, because God from the beginning chose you for salvation through sanctification by the Spirit and belief in the truth, to which He called you by our gospel, for the obtaining of the glory of our Lord Jesus Christ." (2 Thess 2:13–14)

"For to you it has been granted on behalf of Christ, not only to believe in Him, but also to suffer for His sake." (Phil 1:29)

"Therefore do not be ashamed of the testimony of our Lord, nor of me His prisoner, but share with me in the sufferings for the gospel according to the power of God, who has saved us and called us with a holy calling, not according to our works, but according to His own purpose and grace which was given to us in Christ Jesus before time began." (2 Tim 1:8–9)

What Does the Bible Say?

God Elects Individuals to Salvation, Not Just Groups to Service

"For now I have chosen and sanctified this house, that My name may be there forever; and My eyes and My heart will be there perpetually." (2 Chr 7:16)

"Thus says the Lord God of Israel: 'Your fathers, including Terah, the father of Abraham and the father of Nahor, dwelt on the other side of the River in old times; and they served other gods. Then I took your father Abraham from the other side of the River, led him throughout all the land of Canaan, and multiplied his descendants and gave him Isaac.'" (Josh 24:2–3)

"And Jesus came and spoke to them, saying, 'All authority has been given to Me in heaven and on earth. Go therefore and make disciples of all the nations, baptizing them in the name of the Father and of the Son and of the Holy Spirit, teaching them to observe all things that I have commanded you; and lo, I am with you always, even to the end of the age.' Amen." (Matt 28:18–20)

"So when they had eaten breakfast, Jesus said to Simon Peter, 'Simon, son of Jonah, do you love Me more than these?' He said to Him, 'Yes, Lord; You know that I love You.' He said to him, 'Feed My lambs.' He said to him again a second time, 'Simon, son of Jonah, do you love Me?' He said to Him, 'Yes, Lord; You know that I love You.' He said to him, 'Tend My sheep.' He said to him the third time, 'Simon, son of Jonah, do you love Me?' Peter was grieved because He said to him the third time, 'Do you love Me?' And he said to Him, 'Lord, You know all things; You know that I love You.' Jesus said to him, 'Feed My sheep.'" (John 21:15–17)

"Now when the Gentiles heard this, they were glad and glorified the word of the Lord. And as many as had been appointed to eternal life believed." (Acts 13:48)

"But we are bound to give thanks to God always for you, brethren beloved by the Lord, because God from the beginning chose you for salvation through sanctification by the Spirit and belief in the truth." (2 Thess 2:13)

"The Elder, to the elect lady and her children, whom I love in truth, and not only I, but also all those who have known the truth." (2 John 1:1)

References

Aquinas, Thomas. *Summa Theologica*. 2nd and rev. ed. Translated by Fathers of the English Dominican Province. Denver: New Advent, 2017. https://www.newadvent.org/summa/.
Arminius, James. *Arminius Speaks: Essential Writings on Predestination, Free Will, and the Nature of God*. Edited by John D. Wagner. Eugene, OR: Wipf & Stock, 2011.
Augustine, Saint. *Confessions*. Translated by Henry Chadwick. Oxford: Oxford University Press, 1991.
Berkhof, Louis. *The History of Christian Doctrines*. Carlisle, PA: Banner of Truth, 2009.
———. *Systematic Theology*. Eastford, CT: Martino Fine Books, 2020.
Calvin, John. *Commentary on John*. Vol. 1. Grand Rapids: Christian Classics Ethereal Library, n.d. https://www.ccel.org/ccel/calvin/calcom34.html.
———. *Institutes of the Christian Religion*. 1909. Reprint, Budapest: Hungarian Reformed Church, 1995.
Davidson, Bruce W. "Unholy Hate: The Essence of Human Evil in the Theology of Jonathan Edwards." *JETS* 64.4 (2021) 643–55.
Delany, Joseph. "Age of Reason." In *The Catholic Encyclopedia*, vol. 1. New York: Robert Appleton Company, 1907. https://www.newadvent.org/cathen/01209a.htm.
Edwards, Jonathan. *The Works of Jonathan Edwards*. Vol. 1. Revised and corrected by Edward Hickman. Carlisle, PA: Banner of Truth, 1995.
Erdman, Charles R. *The Epistle of Paul to the Ephesians*. Philadelphia, PA: Westminster Press, 1931.
Flowers, Leighton. *God's Providence for All*. Dallas: Trinity Academic, 2019.
———. *The Potter's Promise: A Biblical Defense of Traditional Soteriology*. Dallas: Trinity Academic Press, 2017.
Frassetto, Michael. *The Great Medieval Heretics*. New York: BlueBridge, 2008.
Fritz, Guy: "The Universality of God's Love." In *The Grace of God and the Will of Man*, edited by Clark H. Pinnock, 31–49. Minneapolis: Bethany House, 1989.
Genke, Victor, and Gumerlock, Francis X. *Gottschalk and a Medieval Predestination Controversy*. Milwaukee: Marquette University Press, 2010.
Gill, John. *The Cause of God and Truth*. 1855. Reprint, Fareham, England: Bierton Particular Baptists, n.d.

References

González, Justo. *The Story of Christianity, Volume 2: The Reformation to the Present Day.* San Francisco: HarperCollins, 1985.

Gumerlock, Francis X. "Gottschalk of Orbais: A Medieval Predestinarian." Kerux, Dec 2007. https://kerux.com/doc/2203A4.asp.

Hamilton, Ian. *Salvation, Full and Free in Christ.* Edinburgh: Banner of Truth, 2020.

Henry, Matthew. *Commentary on the Whole Bible.* 1706. Reprint, Richmond: Bible Study Tools, n.d.

Hodge, Charles. *Systematic Theology.* Vol. 2. Grand Rapids: Eerdmans, 1982.

Horton, Michael. *Christless Christianity: The Alternative Gospel of the American Church.* Grand Rapids: Baker, 2008.

Kurzweil, Ray. *How to Create a Mind.* New York: Penguin Books, 2013.

Laney, J. Carl. *A Guide to Church Discipline.* Eugene, OR: Wipf & Stock, 2010.

Lazar, Shawn. *Chosen to Serve: Why Divine Election Is to Service, not to Eternal Life.* Denton, Texas: Grace Evangelical Society, 2017.

Libet, Benjamin. *Mind Time: The Temporal Factor in Consciousness.* Cambridge, MA: Harvard University Press, 2005.

Lightfoot, Joseph Barber, and J. R. Harmer. *The Apostolic Fathers.* 2nd ed. Grand Rapids: Baker, 1989.

Luther, Martin. *The Bondage of the Will.* Ada, MI: Baker Academic, 2012.

Marsden, George M. *Fundamentalism and American Culture.* 2nd ed. Oxford: Oxford University Press, 2006.

Morris, Henry. *The Remarkable Record of Job: The Ancient Wisdom, Scientific Accuracy and Life-Changing Message of an Amazing Book.* Ada, MI: Baker, 1988.

Murray, John. *Redemption Accomplished and Applied.* Grand Rapids: Eerdmans, 1995.

Olson, Roger. *Against Calvinism.* Grand Rapids: Zondervan, 2011.

———. *Arminian Theology: Myths and Realities.* Downer Grove, IL: InterVarsity, 2006.

Owen, John. *A Display of Arminianism.* 1642. Reprint, n.p.: First Rate, 2013.

Peterson, Robert A., and Michael D. Williams. *Why I Am Not an Arminian.* Downers Grove, IL: InterVarsity, 2004.

Pink, Arthur W. *The Life of David.* N.p.: Bottom of the Hill, 2011.

———. *The Sovereignty of God.* 1930. Reprint, Grand Rapids, MI: Baker, 1983.

Piper, John. *Providence.* Wheaton, IL: Crossway, 2021.

Riddlebarger, K. *A Case for Amillenialism: Understanding the End Times.* Grand Rapids: Baker, 2013.

Robertson, O. P. *The Israel of God.* Phillipsburg, NJ: Presbyterian and Reformed Publishing, 2000.

Schaff, Philip, ed. *A Select Library of the Nicene and Post-Nicene Fathers of the Christian Church: Volume III, St. Augustin; On the Holy Trinity, Doctrinal Treatises, Moral Treatises.* Grand Rapids: Eerdmans, 1980.

Smith, M. H. *Systematic Theology.* Vol. 1. Eugene, OR: Wipf & Stock, 2019.

"Soteriology 101 w/ Dr. Leighton Flowers." YouTube, n.d. https://www.youtube.com/channel/UCPRJ7X3hyFvm-3Jo8rVWYOw.

Sproul, R. C. *Chosen by God.* Carol Stream, IL: Tyndale, 1986.

———. *The Righteous Shall Live by Faith, Romans: An Expositional Commentary.* Sanford, FL: Ligonier Ministries, 2019.

———. *Willing to Believe: Understanding the Role of Human Will in Salvation.* Grand Rapids: Baker, 1997.

References

Steele, D. N., et al. *The Five Points of Calvinism Defined, Defended, and Documented.* 2nd ed. Phillipsburg, NJ. Presbyterian and Reformed Publishing, 2004.

Stoyanov, Y. *The Other God.* New Haven, CT: Yale University Press, 2000.

"Strong's #4267." Bible Tools, n.d. https://www.bibletools.org/index.cfm/fuseaction/Lexicon.show/ID/G4267/proginosko.htm.

Tardieu, M. *Manichaeism.* Translated by Malcolm DeBevoise. Chicago, IL: University of Illinois Press, 1997.

Walls, J. L., and J. R. Dongell. *Why I Am Not a Calvinist.* Downers Grove, IL: InterVarsity, 2004.

Warfield, B. B. *Augustine and the Pelagian Controversy: The Doctrines and Theology of Pelagius in the Early Christian Church.* 1897. Reprint, n.p.: Pantianos Classics, n.d.

White, James R. *The Potter's Freedom.* Amityville, NY: Calvary, 2000.

Wilson, Ken. *The Foundation of Augustinian-Calvinism.* Montgomery, TX: Regula Fidei, 2019.

Subject Index

abortion, 28–30
Abraham's sacrifice of Isaac, 27–28
abstinence, 76
Adam, free will and, 32
adoption (*Ordo Salutis* element), 74, 139–40
Against Calvinism (Olson), 48
age of morally responsible, 29n4
Ahab, King of Israel, 55–56
"all" meaning of, 133–38
Ambrose, 3
Ammonites, 80
Amolo of Lyons, 28
Aquinas, Thomas, 2, 6–7
Arians, 11
Arminian Methodists, 6, 67
Arminianism
    creed of, 2
    divine self-limitation, 15
    on evil, 58
    freewill theology, 8, 11
    God's sovereignty, 36
    human will, 30–31
    Manichaeism, 12
    preceptive will, 27
    predestination, 6
    on salvation, 68, 70–72
    semi-Pelagian, 30
    on sinfulness of mankind, 21
    songs of, 20
    sower of the seed parable, 26
    on suffering, 48–49, 61
    unborn babies, 28–29

Arminius, Jacobus (Hermanszoon, Jakob), 94–95
Athanasius, 3
atheism, 22, 108
Augustine, 2–3, 8, 11–15, 100

Basil the Great, 3
Bavinck, Herman, 6, 76
belief, ability of, 100
Berkhof, Louis, 6
Beza, Theodore, 6, 7
biblical anthropology of humans, 21–23
biblical support for Calvinist doctrine
    "all" meaning of, 133–38
    calamity on some people, 128–33
    choice and, 68–70, 84–87, 112–17
    on concurrence, 117–18
    on election, 118–19, 139–40, 141
    Father God, drawing people to himself, 65–68
    foreordain some to hell, 125–27
    God determines all things, 120–21
    God's foreknowledge, 71–73
    inability of man, 121–23
    nature, defines man, not will, 123
    overview, 64
    regeneration, 73–76, 139–40
    Romans 9 and, 76–84
    total depravity, 138–39
    who did Jesus die for, 124–25
    whom does God call to salvation, 119–20, 139–40

Subject Index

Bogomilism, 8, 10
Book of Life, 3n4, 28, 61, 72, 119

calamity on some people, 128–33
calling (*Ordo Salutis* element), 74, 139–40
Calvin, John, 6, 7, 11, 15–17, 93, 99, 100, 103
Calvinism
    appeal to mystery, 91–92
    cause of salvation, 90–91, 94–95
    choice or divine decree, 92–93
    concurrence, doctrine of, 5, 40–45, 54, 83, 104
    on eternality of evil, 12–14, 108–9
    on evangelization, 109–10
    hyper-Calvinism, 40, 106, 110
    on immanence, 105–7
    importance of, 6
    justice, God's, 107–9
    love, God's, 107–9
    power (sovereignty) of God, 107–9, 108n2
    on prayer, 110–11
    straw man argument against, 89–90
    as traditional soteriology, 8
    on transcendence, 105–7
    See also biblical support for Calvinist doctrine
Carey, William, 18, 109
Cassian, John, 99n17
Catharism, 10
celibacy, gift of, 27
chess player analogies, 33–36
choice, God and, 68–70, 84–87, 112–17
Church, tradition and, 2
Clement of Alexandria, 3
Clement of Rome, 3, 3n4
climbing the stairs analogy, 98–99
concurrence, doctrine of, 5, 40–45, 54, 83, 104, 117–18
Confessions (Augustine), 11
conscious free will, 31
conversion (*Ordo Salutis* element), 74
Cottrell, Jack, 15
Council of Carthage (418), 8
Council of Dordt (1618–1619), 6
Council of Ephesus (431), 8
creation, 10, 12, 22, 37, 90, 96, 105, 110

Cserhati, Matthew, 110
Cyprian, 3
Cyril of Jerusalem, 3

Darwin, Charles, 22
David, King of Judah, 53–54
decretive will, 27–28
depravity, 138–39
desires of people, 32
disciples, after the Resurrection, 101–2
divine revelation, 101–2
divine self-limitation, 15
divine truth, 102
double predestination, 5, 86

Edom/Edomites, God's love and, 80
Edwards, Jonathan, 6, 99
effectual call of salvation, 26–30
efficient grace, 81
election
    (*Ordo Salutis* element), 74, 139–40
    biblical support for, 118–19, 141
    degrees of, 83
    teaching of, 2, 75
    See also predestination
Emmaus, road to, 101
Enchiridion (Augustine), 12
Epistle of Barnabas, 4–5
evangelization, 109–10
evil, 12–14, 108–9

faith, 91, 100, 139–40
fall, 10, 12, 15, 32, 71, 101
fallen nature, 32, 91
Father God
    drawing people to himself, 65–68
    sacrifice of the Son, 61–62
Faustus, 11–12
filioque teaching, 11
Flowers, Leighton
    background, 1
    on Calvin, 15–16
    on character of God, 19–20
    God's Provision for All, 99, 101
    plea to reject Calvinism, 87
    The Potter's Promise:, 1, 21
    traditional soteriology, 1–8
foreknowledge, 37–39, 71–73

Subject Index

forgiveness, 91, 94
four angels in Book of Revelation, 22
freewill theology, 6, 8, 11, 13, 24–32, 36, 66n5, 82

general call of salvation, 26–30
glorification (*Ordo Salutis* element), 74, 139–40
Gnosticism, 10
God
    biblical anthropology of humans, 21–23
    calamity on some, 128–33
    character of, 19–23
    choice and, 68–70, 84–87
    determines all things, 120–21
    Father, drawing people to himself, 65–68
    Father's sacrifice of the Son, 61–62
    foreknowledge and, 37–39, 71–73
    foreordain some to hell, 125–27
    grace of. *see* grace of God
    hate for people, 128
    immanence, 77, 105–7
    justice, 107–9
    love and, 107–9
    meaning of "all," 133–38
    omnipotence, 36–37
    power (sovereignty) of, 39–40, 107–9, 108n2
    sovereignty of, 33–36
    transcendence, 77, 105–7
    understanding through, 101–2
    See also Holy Spirit; Jesus
God's Provision for All (Flowers), 23, 99, 101
Gottschalk of Orbais, 5–6, 28, 100
grace of God
    abuse of, 51
    cause of salvation, 26, 90–91
    divine truth and, 101
    efficient grace, 81
    everything due to, 70
    prevenient grace, 30, 67
Gregorius Nazianzenus, 3

Hamilton, Ian, 94

hate for people, 128
Hermanszoon, Jakob (Jacobus Arminius), 94–95
Hilarius Diaconus, 3
Hilarius Pictaviensis, 3
Hodge, Charles, 6, 35
Holy Spirit, 2, 7–8, 26, 93, 97, 102–4
human will, 30–32
humility, 17, 93, 96–98
Hungary, historical tumults, 39
hyper-Calvinism, 40, 106, 110

Ignatius, 3, 5
inability of man, 121–23
Institutes (Calvin), 15, 93
Irenaeus of Lyons, 3, 5
Isaac, 27–28, 80
Ishmaelites, 80
Islam, 10, 35

Jehoiachin, King of Judah, 60
Jehoshaphat, King of Judah, 55
Jehovah's Witnesses, 11
Jerusalem, fall of, 60–61
Jesus, 2, 41, 61–62, 65–67, 101–2, 124–25
Job's suffering, 56–58
Joseph sole into slavery, 52–53
Judas, betrayer of Jesus, 21, 41, 58, 61, 86
judicial hardening
    David, King of Judah, 53–54
    fall of Jerusalem, 60–61
    Father's sacrifice of the Son, 61–62
    Job's suffering, 56–58
    Joseph sole into slavery, 52–53
    Moses and Pharaoh, 52
    overview, 48–52
    Paul's throne in the flesh, 62–63
    prophets' mouths, lying spirit in, 55–56
    Roboam, suffering and, 59
Judson, Adinoram, 109
justification, 11, 97, 129–40
justification (*Ordo Salutis* element), 74
Justin Martyr, 3, 5

Letter to Diognetus, 5
libertarian freedom, 34, 35n5

Subject Index

Libet, Benjamin, 31
Livingstone, David, 18, 109
lost coin parable, 44, 83, 95
lost sheep parable, 44, 83, 95
Lot, as righteous, 80
Luther, Martin, 6, 7, 100, 103

Mani (self-proclaimed prophet), 8–9
Manichaeism, 8–10, 71, 108
Marcionism, 10
mercy of God
    Calvin on, 93
    election and, 16–17, 69
    Gottschalk on, 6
    to the humble, 95–96
    as infinite, 51
    Isaiah on, 121
    said to Moses, 64, 80, 115
    Timothy on, 116
    vessels of, 83, 115, 140
messianic secret, 46–48
Methodists, 6, 67
Micaiah, prophet, 55
Minutius Felix, 3
Moabites, 80
Montanists, 3n6
Morrison, Robert, 18
Moses, the Egyptian exit, 22, 26, 41–42, 52
motives of people, 32

nature, defines man, not will, 123
Nebuchadnezzar, King of Babylon, 60
Nicodemus, the Pharisee, 75
Novatianus, 3

Olson, Roger, 15, 30–31, 48–49, 95
omnipotence, 36–37
On Predestination (Gottschalk), 6
open theism, 34
ordo salutis, 70n14, 73–76, 93, 139–40
Origen of Alexandria, 3, 5
original sin, 29–30, 51, 101, 103
Owens, John, 6

Paul's throne in the flesh, 62–63
Pelagius/Pelagianism, 5, 6, 28–29, 94, 98, 100

perseverance (*Ordo Salutis* element), 74, 139–40
Peterson, Robert A., 91
Pharaoh, the Egyptian exit, 22, 26, 41–44, 52
Pink, Arthur, 31, 98
Piper, John, 20, 48
Polycarp, 3–4, 5
The Potter's Freedom (White), 1, 33
The Potter's Promise (Flowers), 1, 21
prayer, Calvinism on, 110–11
preceptive will, 27–28
predestination
    foreordain some to hell, 125–27
    Gottschalk on, 6
    See also election
prevenient grace, 30, 67
prodigal son parable, 44–45, 83, 94
prophets' mouths, lying spirit in, 55–56
Provisionists, 13

Reformed theology, 26, 110
regeneration, 73–76, 139–40
remonstrant theology, 6
repentance (*Ordo Salutis* element), 74
reprobation, doctrine of, 27, 48
responsibility, bible on, 95–98
rider of the red horse, in Book of Revelation, 57
Roboam, suffering and, 59
Roman Catholic Church, 2, 7, 29n4, 30, 97, 106
Romans 9, support Calvinist worldview, 76–84

sacerdotalism, 11
salvation
    general and effectual call of, 26–30
    by God's grace, 25–26, 70
    stages in, 70n14
    whom does God call to, 119–20
sanctification (*Ordo Salutis* element), 74, 97, 139–40
Satan, 12–14, 49–51, 57–58, 108
Schaff, Philip, 32
Second Council of Orange (529), 8
semi-Pelagianism, 5, 30, 94, 99n17
service, chosen for, 84–87

Subject Index

should implies could argument, 98–104
sins
    consequences, 51
    original sin, 29–30, 51, 101, 103
    punishment and, 107–8
sixth trumpet in Book of Revelation, 22
Solomon, King of Israel, 59
songs, theological accuracy of, 19, 20n2
sovereignty
    foreknowledge, 37–39, 71–73
    of God, 33–36
    omnipotence and, 36–37
sower of the seed parable, 26, 102
Sproul, R. C., 6, 100
Spurgeon, Charles, 6
suffering, 48–50, 54, 56–59
Summa Theologica (Aquinas), 6–7

Tardieu, M., 9
Taylor, J. Hudson, 18, 109
Tertullian, 3, 3n6, 5
Thomas (apostle), 8
total depravity, 138–39
traditionalism, 1–8
transcendence, 77, 105–7

Trinity, doctrine of, 11, 40–41
TULIP (acronym), 6
tumults of history, 39–40

unborn babies, 28–30, 79, 79n32
understanding Jesus, 101–2
Unitarians, 11
universalism, 25

von Hutten, Ulrich, 7

Warfield, B. B., 12
Washington, George, 17
wedding banquet example, 24–25
Wesley, John, 67
Wesleyan Arminianism, 30
Westminster Confession, 29, 34–35
Westminster Shorter Catechism, 97
White, James, 1, 6, 31
Williams, Michael D., 91
Wilson, Ken, 4–5
Wycliffe of England, 6

Zwingli, Huldrych, 7

Scripture Index

OLD TESTAMENT

Genesis
6:5	138
6:5–7	128
12:3	87, 133
15:12	112
15:17	112
17:20	80
22:1–19	27
37	52
39:20	52
39:23	52
45:5–8	52
50:20	46, 50, 109

Exodus
4:11	128
4:21	22, 26, 41, 42
7:3	22, 42, 121
7:13	42, 121
7:19	133
8:15	42, 121
8:19	42
8:32	42, 122
9:7	42
9:12	22, 42, 122
9:27–30	42
10:1	22, 122
10:16–18	43
10:20	22, 43, 122
10:27	22, 122
11:10	22, 122
14:4	22, 44, 122
14:8	22, 44, 122
14:13–14	90
14:17	22
14:17–18	128
14:27	22
33:19	112

Leviticus
26:17	128, 129

Numbers
23:19	123

Deuteronomy
8:16	129
23:3	80
23:7	80
29:4	27, 125
30:6	27

Joshua
24:2–3	141

Judges
2:15	129

Scripture Index

Ruth
1:4	80

1 Samuel
2:7	129

2 Samuel
15:25–26	129
19:9	133
24:1	129
24:1–2	53
24:10	54, 129

1 Kings
9:9	129
11:1—12:24	59
11:2	59
11:7	59
11:12–13	59
11:35	59
11:39	59
12:4–5	59
12:7	59
12:18	133
12:21	133
17:20	129
18:19	133
19:18	118
20:42	129
21:21	130
21:29	130
22:1–40	55
22:19–23	55
22:30–33	138

2 Kings
6:33	130
7:1–2	108
7:18–20	108
10:32	117, 130
11:1–2	134
11:18	134
21:12	130
22:16	130
22:19	95
24:2	60
24:2–3	130
24:19—25:30	60
24:19–20	60
24:20	60

2 Chronicles
7:16	84, 141
12:7	95
12:12	95
15:6	130
20:5	134
20:13	134
20:17	113
21:16	130
22:7	130
22:10–11	134

Ezra
1:2	134

Job
1:9–11	57
1:21	131
2:9–10	58
2:10	131
14:4	92, 123, 138
18:18	134
21:30	125
42:12–17	58

Psalms
2	23
7:11	87, 128
9:5	126
9:8	134
11:5–6	128
18:27	95
22:27	134
25:9	96
27:23	106
33:11	120
37:23	82, 117
44:2–3	117

Scripture Index

49:21	12	45:4	113
51:5	29	45:7	48, 131
56:5	138	45:8	113
58:3	123	46:9–11	121
76:12	131	53:8	124
80:18	113	53:10	50, 61, 131
81:12	126	53:11–12	124
86:11	82, 117	54:9–10	121
96:13	134	54:13	66
110:3	32, 113	55:11	47
115	36	57:17	131
119:113	82	65:1	113
119:133	117	65:24	121
135:6	34, 121	66:2	96
147:6	96	66:4	55

Proverbs

1:26	131
3:34	96
4:23	31
5:8–9	128
16:1	5, 40, 41, 82, 106, 117
16:4	100, 126
16:33	34, 101, 121
21:1	40, 41, 82, 106, 117
27:6	110

Ecclesiastes

1:9	8
7:20	113

Song of Songs

1:4	66, 113
1:37	67
1:39	67
1:44	67

Isaiah

6:9–10	126
13:11	134
24:21	37
26:9	135
34:5	131

Jeremiah

3:6–10	78
13:23	92
17:9	21, 44, 96
18:1–6	82, 83
18:3–6	113
18:8	131
18:11	131
31:18	113

Lamentations

2:14	56
3:38	131

Ezekiel

36:26	75, 122
37:11	138

Daniel

1	60
1:8–20	60
1:14	60
1:17	61
7:6	50
7:12	50
7:21	50
7:26	50

Scripture Index

Hosea
2:21—3:1	84

Joel
2:11	16

Amos
3:2	131

Zephaniah
2:3	96

Malachi
1:2–3	113
3:6	2

NEW TESTAMENT

Matthew
1:5	80
1:21	124
3:5	135
4:8–9	57
5:3	96
5:5	98
5:11–12	105
5:12	95
5:45	20, 51, 87
5:48	28
6:5–7	111
7:17–18	86
10:29	132
11:5	76
11:12–15	26
11:14–15	119
12:11	27
13:3–9	26
13:9	76
13:9–11	119
13:11	74, 118
13:20–21	25, 86
16	102
16:2–0	46
16:17	102
16:21–23	50
18:4	96
19:11	27, 119
19:26	103
20:10–16	118
20:23	38
20:28	47, 124
22	25
22:1–14	24
22:11–14	120
23:12	96
26:28	124
26:39	132
26:41	111
27:3–4	41
27:4	104, 131
28:18–20	85, 141
28:19–20	109

Mark
1:5	135
3:12	46
4:9	26, 74, 104
4:9–11	120
4:9–12	102
4:23	27, 120
7:21	31
8:30	46
9:9	46
10:17–22	96
10:25–27	97
14:24	124

Luke
1:52	96
2:1	135
4:6	49, 57
8:8	26, 74
8:8–10	120
10:20	16, 118
14:11	96
14:35	27, 120
15:4–7	44
15:8–9	114
15:8–10	44
15:11:32	44

156

15:17–19	45	12:32	68, 135
18:14	96	12:39–40	126
19:39–40	118	12:47	135
21:24	135	14:2–3	38
22:22	61	14:6	29
22:31	50	14:12	83
22:31–32	58	14:16–17	122
24:13–35	101	14:22	135
24:31	74	15:5	91, 103, 114
24:36–49	101	15:13	124
24:45	74	15:16	24, 25, 72, 86, 114
		15:18	138
		15:18–19	135

John

1:10–11	138	15:19	114
1:11	47, 84	15:26	105
1:12	95	16:13	2
1:12–13	75, 122	17:2	119
3:3	75	17:6	119
3:3–8	74	17:9	47, 124
3:7–8	139	17:12	21, 86, 104, 126
3:8	26, 114	17:14	136
3:16	68, 100	17:24	124
3:18	100, 126	18:8–9	125
3:27	27, 114	19:11	27, 132
4:39	135	19:29	136
5:21	118	21:15–17	85, 141
6	64		
6:35	66		

Acts

6:37	66, 68, 106, 117, 139	2:14–38	85
		2:17a	136
6:37–39	74	2:22–23	41
6:37–46	65, 66, 68, 69	2:23	61, 104
6:44	26, 114, 140	2:28	26
6:45	65n2, 68	4:27–28	34
6:63	74, 102	8:22	114
6:64–65	74, 114	8:22–23	91
6:70	21, 86, 126	11:18	89, 91, 115
7:2–5	47	13:48	66, 66n5, 75, 140, 141
7:7	135		
8:36	32, 114	17:25	136
8:44	114, 123	17:26	40
8:47	119, 126	17:28	105, 121
9:39	126	17:30–31	106
10:11	124	19:27	136
10:26	100, 126	20:28	125
10:29	119	21:13–14	132
12:19	135	26:4–5	72

Scripture Index

Romans

1:8	136
1:17	103
1:20	103
1:20–21	22
1:21–22	56
1:21–23	22
1:24–28	127
2:5–6	51
3:1–2	84
3:10–12	115, 139
3:11	32, 75
3:11–12	99
3:12	21
3:26	140
3:28	140
3:30	140
4:4	94
5:1–11	74
5:3–4	74
5:10	100
5:14	103
5:17	103
5:19	103
6:20	139
8	71
8–9	64
8:5	103
8:5–8	97
8:6–8	122
8:8	75
8:14–17	74
8:28	52
8:28–30	74
8:29	71–72, 97
8:29–30	140
8:30	72, 73, 74
8:32	125, 136
9	77
9:6	78, 136
9:9–13	79
9:11	79
9:13	128
9:14–16	64
9:15	96
9:15–16	115
9:15–19	80–81
9:16	32, 74
9:19	115
9:20–23	81, 82, 83
9:21	115, 127
9:22	100
9:23	83, 115, 140
9:23–24	83
9:25–33	84
9:27	84
10:5	94, 95
10:17	28
10:20	84, 115
11:5	78, 84
11:5–6	17
11:8	27, 127
11:15	136
11:25–26	78
12:1–2	96
12:3	92, 115
13:1	66n5

1 Corinthians

1:31	93
2:7–8	46
2:14	97, 103, 123, 139
3:6–7	115
4:4	139
4:7	75, 92, 115
5:19	136
6:2	136
6:12	136
6:20	115
12:6	136
12:11	83
12:12	74
12:14	74
12:20	83
15:24	37

2 Corinthians

2:15	28, 127
3:17	97
4:3	28
4:3–4	123
4:4	57
5:15	127

158

Scripture Index

5:17	96
7:10	43
7:34	43
10:5	116
12:7–10	62

Galatians

1:15	116
2:20	125
3:23–25	100
5:22–23	76, 123
6:16	78

Ephesians

1	64
1:3–4	19
1:3–14	68
1:4	19, 69, 104, 106
1:4–5	140
1:5	69, 74
1:6	74
1:9	69
1:11	6, 33, 34, 38, 69, 74, 121
2:1–10	69–70
2:3	123
2:8	4, 30, 106
2:8–9	90, 116
2:8–10	26
2:9	93
5:25	125
6:12	37
6:21	137
8:8–10	70

Philippians

1:6	111, 116
1:29	140
2:12–13	40, 41, 82, 106, 116, 118
3:19–20	119
4:3	3n4

Colossians

2:13	139
2:20	37

1 Thessalonians

1:4	119
5:23–24	74

2 Thessalonians

1:6–9	132
2:6–7	117
2:11	55, 132
2:13	97, 116, 127, 141
2:13–14	140
2:15	2

1 Timothy

1:15	83
2:1–2	137
4:10	125

2 Timothy

1:8–9	116, 140
1:18	116
2:20	83
2:20–21	82, 83, 118
2:24–26	116
4:7–8	95

Titus

1:2	123

Hebrews

2:17	119
3:10–11	128
3:16–18	137
4:15	61
9:28	125
10:31	16
11:17	125
12:1	8, 71
13:8	38, 87
13.8	2

Scripture Index

James
1:17	2
1:18	117
4:6	96
4:10	96

1 Peter
1:15–16	28
1:22	74
1:23	74
5:5–6	96

2 Peter
1:10	116
2:1–3	127
2:7	80

1 John
2:19	74
3:13	137
4:4–5	137
5:1	74, 75
5:19	137
5:20	117

2 John
1:1	77, 141

Jude
1:4	127

Revelation
2:7	27, 120
2:10	95
2:11	27
2:17	27
2:29	27
3:6	27
3:10	137
3:13	27, 120
3:22	27, 120
6:4	57, 132
6:8	57
6:11	125
9:13–21	22
9:20–21	22
11:4–6	139
11:4–7	132
12:9	137
13:3	137, 139
13:7	57, 133
13:8	61, 72
16:14	138
18:6	133
19:7–8	120
20:7	51
20:12	119
21:24	138
22:11	51

QUR'AN, SURAH

2:106	39n10

www.ingramcontent.com/pod-product-compliance
Lightning Source LLC
Chambersburg PA
CBHW060820190426
43197CB00038B/2163